Looking Good
Feeling Great

Looking Good Good
Feeling Great

Karol Kuhn Truman
With Alan Parkinson

Olympus Distributing

Karol Kuhn Truman

Looking Good Feeling Great
Copyright 1982 Information Design, Inc.

Published by Olympus Distributing
P.O. Box 97693, Las Vegas, Nevada 89193-7693
All rights reserved. Printed in the U.S.A.
Third Printing

Truman, Karol Kuhn–
Healing Feelings . . . From Your Heart
Feelings Buried Alive Never Die . . .
Looking Good Feeling Great
1. Physical Fitness 2. Exercise 3. Health

ISBN: 0-911207-00-7

Contents

Why This Book Was Written

When I was a teenager, like all teenage girls I really wanted a beautiful figure. Even though I wasn't totally beyond hope (no one is!), there was much about my looks that made me unhappy. My hips, for example, held too great a concentration of body mass. My legs suffered from varicose veins. And that was only the beginning of my concerns.

As I grew older, those problems didn't do a great deal to correct themselves. And I found myself gradually going more and more out of shape. But I wasn't alone with my problems:

- I met a high-school friend whom I hadn't seen for at least ten years. She must have gained fifty pounds. She told me she was embarrassed by her looks, but she didn't know what to do about it. She'd tried dieting time after time, always to no avail. To complicate her situation, she said she never felt *really good* anymore. "I don't feel sick, exactly," she said. "But I never feel particularly well, either."

- A neighbor who was still in his early forties had a heart attack that nearly took his life. His cardiologist said that he'd just let himself go too far. "The body can take only so much abuse without needed conditioning," the doctor

1

said. "We can push it and push it, but the time comes when we can't push anymore. Then we either get in shape or face dying." That wasn't a very pleasant thing to hear, but my neighbor needed to hear it.

- A close friend who lived a few blocks away was the mother of five. With each new child she'd put on a little more weight and lose a little more muscle tone. Her tummy began to sag. And the added weight began to show in her cheeks, her chin, her arms. "I'd exercise to get back in shape," she told me. "But I'm just too tired."

I'm convinced we're all suffering from the same problem: we live in a sedentary world (at least compared with the lives people led 100 or 200 or 1,000 years ago), and that world is taking its toll. Nutrition is better today than ever before. Medical science has made advances. Our life-spans have increased. But has the quality of our living improved? Are we taking care of ourselves so we can enjoy all those years of our lives?

In the last few years, people seem to have become more health-conscious. But for many of us it's been simply a concern, rather than a way of life.

I thought about these things and decided I should make some changes in my life. I wanted to look better and feel better. What were my options? I tried jogging, but it was so boring I couldn't keep it up. Swimming is an excellent exercise, but I had to pay weekly or annual fees. Racquetball needs a consistent partner—and it's not as aerobically helpful as some other exercises.

What I needed was something that was easy, something I could do at home, something that brought results, something that didn't require a partner, something that didn't require weekly or annual fees. It might sound like I was asking for the impossible. And maybe I was. But then rebounding was developed. Trampolines had been shown to give great conditioning benefits. Why couldn't mini-trampolines do the same?

When I learned about rebounding, I said "That's what I need!" It was easy and fun to use. I could do it at home. Once I paid for the unit initially, I'd never have to pay again.

I didn't need a partner. I could even do it to music, or while watching the nightly news on television.

I've been rebounding for several years now, and the results were exactly what I'd hoped. Now people come up to me and say, "Hey, you're really looking good!" I just smile and say, "I'm really feeling good, too."

That's what this book is all about. It tells how any of us—all of us—can enjoy the benefits of rebounding. **Rebounding is an exercise that conditions every part of the body, inside and out.** It will slim the thighs, trim the hips, flatten the tummy, firm the bustline, and even refine the face. (For a more complete listing of the ways in which rebounding will help you, review the contents pages of this book.)

How can you get the most out of this book? I'd recommend that you first read it through, cover to cover, just to get an idea of all the benefits you can receive. Then you may want to go through the book again, this time marking the specific things you're concerned about.

Rebounding is a wonder exercise. It helps us take off excess weight and tone up the muscles. It seems to know just what the body needs, then gives it. Want to be looking good and feeling great? Read on!

You Say You Used to Be Thin and Trim?

There I was at my high school reunion. I remember how everyone looked—and how they'd changed from how they used to look in "the good old days."

The first person I ran into was my old friend, Ellen. I hadn't seen her for at least ten years, but she looked just great. Her complexion was rosy, she was trim, her smile was radiant, and she was dressed to perfection. She glowed with health and seemed to light up the room.

The next person I noticed was Fran. She had been one of the elite at school: head cheerleader, always popular with both boys and girls because of her good looks and friendly personality. But now Fran looked—well, to be honest— rather dumpy. She was overweight, her hair lacked luster, and when she spoke she sounded tired.

After the reunion, I went home and took a good look at myself in the mirror. How did I look *to them?*

Gaining weight and/or becoming run-down physically is usually a natural by-product of age, lifestyle, and circumstances—but it doesn't have to be that way! A good exercise program can work wonders with any of us. And I have found rebounding to be the easiest and most fun exercise **with the greatest return of results for time invested.**

Our bodies are in a constant state of change. As time marches on, the degenerating process moves in, and most of the resulting changes aren't for the better. But there's still hope for all of us! We can keep up with that constant rate of change with a constant rate of exercise. We can *counterbalance* the effects of time. Then when you or I go to our next reunions, *we'll* be the one everyone's looking at with envy.

Recently I saw my uncle for the first time since he had changed jobs a few months earlier. With his former job, my uncle had always stayed physically active, was in good health, trim, and looked great. But, I was sad to see, that's not how he looks now. With his change of jobs has come a dramatic change in his physical condition. He's a bit saggy around the middle, his skin color isn't healthy—he just isn't the same vibrant man I have known all these years. And, saddest of all, he doesn't seem to be aware of what has been happening to him. The change has been so gradual that he hasn't even noticed. But I certainly did!

This didn't have to happen. If my uncle had kept up a consistent physical fitness program, he'd still be in great shape.

I know another man, George M., who found himself in the same fix. But he finally realized what was happening, and decided to do something about it.

George worked in an office, and the years at a desk were starting to take their toll. One morning he looked at himself in the mirror and didn't like what he saw. "This is it," he muttered to himself. "This time I'm going to do something that will make a difference!"

He investigated a bit, comparing different kinds of exercise programs. When he finally discovered rebounding, he knew he'd found his answer. He could tell it would be easy and enjoyable. What more could a person ask?

George got started on a regular rebound program and stuck with it. Just three months later when he put on his pants in the morning, he couldn't cinch up the belt—he'd become so slender that the belt was now way too big.

George made some new holes in that old belt and kept on rebounding!

The more George exercised, the more pleased he became—and with good reason. Anybody who takes the trouble to get into shape deserves to be pleased. George was so excited about his success that he started selling rebound units on the side. And you couldn't ask for a better salesman. He wore his old pants and his old belt—which now had about five inches extra—just to show people what rebounding had done for him.

What rebounding did for George, it will do for anyone who gets going with a good consistent program on a quality unit. Those who do try it will find that they're winning their battle against "the ravages of time"!

So what do you have to do? Only fifteen to thirty minutes of rebounding a day—that's all it takes! It's fun, it's easy, and everyone will notice the great change in *you*. If you're thin, your figure will fill out in all the right places; if you're overweight, you'll lose it in the right places. Whatever your build, rebounding will help you to attain and *maintain* the ideal condition for you.

Then, when people ask you how old you are, you can smile and say to yourself, "My age? What does age matter? Just look at me!"

Dieting Can Be Torture—Are You Tired of Torturing Yourself?

Here are some of the frustrations we've all heard from dieters:

- "I feel cranky all the time."
- "My thoughts are all of FOOD—I *crave* food!"
- "I get really sneaky and try to find all kinds of ways to get a little extra bite everywhere I can. Then I jump whenever anyone enters the room and I'm caught eating."
- "I just feel frustrated about everything."
- "I get so tired."
- "It never works the way I want it to—I lose weight, but in all the wrong places."
- "I go along really well for a week or so, and then I gain back everything I've lost in a couple of days. It's so depressing!"
- "I feel *weak*, physically and mentally."
- "The only things I'm allowed to eat are so *boring* and not satisfying at all. I have hunger pangs all day, no matter how much I eat."

Dieting is a pretty frustrating experience, isn't it? Yes, you may get results eventually, but in the meantime it's a war

7

between you and your will-power—until discouragement sets in. Then the war's over—but neither side has won. No wonder so many people are always dieting, but seldom keeping the lost weight off.

Happily, there are other options. Let me tell you of a lady named Laurie H. When she went to her doctor for a routine checkup, he determined she was in fairly good condition—except she needed to lose a little weight. He recommended that she begin an exercise program. Notice that he *didn't* tell her to start dieting. He told her to *exercise*.

Laurie had owned a rebound unit for about a year, but she hadn't really used it. She decided to follow her doctor's advice and give it a try. Already an active person, Laurie decided to dedicate at least twenty minutes a day to concentrated rebound exercise. She also made another important commitment: no sweets. Within two weeks' time she'd lost fifteen pounds. She has now increased her efforts to thirty minutes a day—and she constantly gets comments on her trim shape, vitality, and endurance:

"You're so radiant—how do you do it?"

"Every week you seem to look better!"

"I wish I could keep my weight down like you."

"You're one of the most attractive women I know."

Of course, Laurie has a little secret. She knows how to use her rebound unit to keep that ideal figure. And now she feels better about herself. She's a joy to be around, because she's so cheerful and happy. And now she's able to eat anything she wants!

Dieting is an inefficient and unpleasant way to control weight.

An interesting experiment was performed in 1944. A group of volunteers were isolated in the University of Minnesota dormitories and subjected to a series of tests to determine the effects of hunger. For the first two months, a good diet and exercise program was followed, and the volunteers became quite healthy. Then the testers began to gradually starve them.

The calorie intake was cut in half and the people began to lose weight. An attempt to continue the exercise program was made, but the volunteers became lethargic and unproductive. In addition, they became quarrelsome and negative with one another. They lost interest in taking care of their rooms and other quarters. This apathy began to show in the way they cared for themselves as well; the volunteers quit grooming their hair, brushing their teeth, etc.

At mealtimes, they played with their food, spiced it heavily, mixed it around, and made the meal—even though a small one—last up to a couple of hours in order to savor and enjoy each meager bite. They began to think about food constantly and much of their time was taken up with daydreams about it.

When the experiment was over, most of the volunteers went on eating binges. They gained back all the weight they had lost and more; most kept this extra weight for the rest of their lives.

This is the way people react to hunger—and the way most people react to dieting. Dieting—as most of us do it—just doesn't work on a lasting basis. And it makes you feel miserable while you're doing it.

Sensible dieting (cutting down the calorie intake of foods that are not nutritious) is another matter. When it is accompanied by a consistent exercise program, moderate dieting has pleasant, long-lasting results. It's a program a person can live with. And once the excess weight is off, maintenance of the exercise program enables most people to keep their weight at an ideal level even though they might allow their caloric intake to increase some.

So take a tip from Laurie, and remember that thirty minutes of exercise a day keeps the pounds *and dieting frowns* away.

No Easier Way to Get in Shape and Stay in Shape

How to Use This Book

You say you really believe that exercising is the thing you should do, but you just don't have the time? Then I think rebounding is for you.

You're a homemaker with preschool-age children at home and no car or extra money? Then rebounding is for you.

You're a career woman with such a heavy schedule that you can't even fit in your social life? Rebounding is something you *can* fit in.

You don't want the hassle of going outdoors after dark and in all kinds of weather—even though you've tried jogging and know how good it makes you feel? Then I'd suggest you try rebounding.

You're suffering from the pains of shin splints and jogger's ankles, but you still want to exercise aerobically? Then rebounding is what you need!

You're too tired after a hard day's work to do the exercising you know you should do? Then your answer is rebounding.

You wish you could find an exercise program that helps you in specific areas and will give great all-around results at the same time? You've come to the right place!

For years I've looked around at the exercise approaches we have available to us—and I've come to the conclusion that *no* exercise program is more convenient, effective, or *easier* than rebounding. And I've found no exercise that's more fun, exhilarating, and pleasant for everyone!

I think it's very interesting to listen to members of the medical profession, and to hear them confess what they've most neglected in the past few years: *preventive medicine*. Until recently, doctors have been so busy *treating* diseases that they haven't spent much time giving emphasis to those things that would help *prevent* diseases.

Now things are changing. Read any family-type or women's magazine today and you'll find at least one article—usually more—about exercise and/or nutrition. We are finally waking up! What could be a simpler approach to health and happiness than good nutrition and effective exercise? These two things will help our bodies work at peak condition, produce the energy and feeling of well-being that we need in order to face our responsibilities, and hinder disease and deterioration. In addition, they'll make us feel more radiant and lovely, in the inner sense, than we've ever felt before.

I believe in exercise, in keeping our bodies in good shape, and I care about the general health of the public. And I care about *you!* That's what this book is all about. Of all the exercise programs I've tried, my rebound unit has brought me the *best* results with the *least* amount of trouble, money, or risk. It's helped me to feel better mentally and physically, feel better inside, look better outside, and have more energy than ever before. So I'm taking this opportunity to tell you all about rebounding—what it can do for you, how it does it, and why I really think you should try it.

This book has been designed to serve you, the reader. All the stories you will read are true—actual accounts of what has happened to different people as they put rebounding to work for them. The names of individiuals have been changed in order to maintain their privacy, but the facts are simply that: facts. They are actual occurrences in the lives of those who want to share their enthusiasm for rebounding with you.

I've tried to write this book so you could use it any way you want to: read it cover to cover like a novel, to see how all the pieces fit together; or use it like a cookbook or dictionary, looking up only those areas that you need at a particular time. Just like rebounding itself, *Looking Good, Feeling Great* has been designed to be convenient, flexible, and easy to use. Since each section can stand alone, giving you all the information you need about a certain topic, the book is easy to get into and the information is easily accessible.

I do recommend that you at some time read the entire book. You may find that rebounding can help you in ways you never dreamed possible. Again, this book is just like rebounding itself: you *may* exercise for the specific purpose of slimming your hips, for example. But at the same time, exercise on the rebound unit is strengthening and conditioning *your whole body*. With this book, you *may* just look up a specific section, read it, and leave it at that for the time being. But if you read the whole book, you'll gain greater understanding of the whole rebound program and how it works for you.

My greatest hope is that this book will change your life, just as its ideas have changed mine. Rebounding is one of the greatest things that's ever happened to me, and I'm grateful for the chance I have to share it with you. I know that rebounding will give you more than you dreamed an exercise program could ever give!

Important—Read This

As with any exercise program, it is wise to check with your doctor and know your physical condition before beginning. And I advise you to always be careful not to overexert yourself. Overexertion can lead to injury, as well as to discouragement over sore muscles.

An attorney friend of mine, David M., decided one day to try rebounding. He had never used the unit before, but he got on it and began exercising—vigorously. The next day he woke up with a sore back; he had aggravated an old injury. It hurt so much that he figured the rebound unit was to blame—and he swore he wouldn't use it again.

Two or three months passed. One day David mentioned that he'd been having trouble sleeping. "My back hurts," he complained. "It doesn't matter how I sleep—front, back, or side—it still hurts like crazy when I wake up in the morning. And the dozen times I wake up during the night."

"You ought to use your rebound unit every night," I said. "Just a few minutes to get rid of some of your tension would be all you'd need."

He wasn't too sure about using his unit again, but he was ready to try anything. This time he followed instructions, and exercised gently, less than five minutes each time—and this solved his back problem, without creating any new problems.

The first time David rebounded, he hurt his back and blamed the rebound unit. But it wasn't to blame at all. The real problem was his impulsive *overexertion*.

The second time he exercised, he started slowly and lightly, increasing the exercise only gradually throughout a succession of days. It did for him everything he wanted.

Another example is my friend, Rosemary K. The first time she began using a rebound unit she lasted about two minutes. Then she began to complain of a very bad headache. Her problem was that she was so out of condition that as she started jumping it stimulated the circulation, which was too great a strain on those unconditioned cells. If she had started out slowly and lightly, and for only a short period of time, her cells would have had time to gradually accustom themselves to being toned. She would then have felt the *good* feelings that come from a gradual, consistent conditioning and not the unpleasant effects of overexertion.

But even before you start your exercise program (slow and easy!), you need to do something else: consult your physician. I'm talking to everyone here, but especially to those with any kind of heart problem and those who have a history of physical troubles.

It is all too common for people to have heart attacks by overexerting themselves physically. So please, please be certain that you don't have any problems—or, if you do, that your doctor knows what your exercise program is and has given you the go-ahead.

Now, the likelihood of any injury while using a rebound unit is very slight. But it can happen. Wisdom dictates that you follow these precautions before beginning *any* strenuous physical activities:

1. **Start slowly and easily.** "Rome was not built in a day"—and neither is a healthy body. Give those unconditioned cells a chance to "warm up," to become accustomed to the stress you're putting on them. You'll discover that if you treat your body with respect, it will perform beautifully for you. (To learn where to start with your rebound unit, see the "Beginning Program" section and follow the steps outlined.)

14

2. **Consult your physician**, especially if you have any questions concerning your physical and health status.

3. **Check your heart rate to determine your present condition.** This knowledge will help guard against overexertion.

4. **Keep your balance.** Don't get fancy on the rebound unit and try to touch the ceiling or do other circus tricks. Use a steady, reasonable bounce and "spot" something stationary with your eyes. Why? As your body moves up and down, your eyes move also in order to maintain the focal point. If you keep a point of focus, you'll enjoy better equilibrium.

Checking Your Heart Rate to Determine Your Present Condition

In beginning an exercise program, there are three types of heart rates you need to determine:

1. Resting heart rate. This is an indication of your current fitness status.

2. Maximum heart rate. This is the highest rate your heart can attain.

3. Training zone heart rate. This is the heart rate you should maintain during an exercise period in order to get the most efficient and effective results from your program.

This section deals with the resting heart rate only. The others are treated in a heart rate chart at the back of the book.

The ideal time to take your resting pulse is before your feet hit the floor in the morning. While lying in bed, place your index and middle fingers on the thumb side of your inner wrist or gently at the side of your neck, just under your jaw. Using the sweep-second hand of your watch, count your heartbeats for thirty seconds. Multiply the number by two to determine your pulse rate for one minute. This is your resting rate.

Women average 75 to 80 beats per minute, girls 82 to 89 beats; men average 72-76 beats per minute, boys 80 to 84. (Medical experts aren't quite sure why females have a slightly higher rate than males.) Remember that these rates are average, and rates as low as 50 and as high as 100 beats per minute can still be considered normal.

Generally, the lower your resting heart rate, the healthier you are. Rates higher than 80 beats per minute usually indicate poor health and fitness, and a higher risk of heart disease and early death. The mortality rate for those with heart rates over 92 is four times greater than for those whose rates are below 67.

As you exercise consistently there should be a noticeable change in your resting heart rate, and I recommend that you recheck it periodically. As the rate decreases, it is an indication that your heart is becoming stronger. However, if your heart rate at the beginning of your exercise program is low, this doesn't mean you can immediately go out and run two miles. Your heart must be conditioned gradually, whether it starts out high or low.

Now I want to give you a few warnings. If you've begun your exercise program and you start to experience any of the following symptoms during or after your exercise, please see your doctor before continuing any program:

- Chest pains
- Consistent problems with light-headedness, dizziness, or fainting
- Consistent problems with gastrointestinal distress
- Extreme difficulty in breathing

If you are more than twenty pounds overweight, or if you are over 35 years of age, you are most likely out of shape right now. You probably don't need me to tell you that it's much easier for you to overexert than for your slimmer or younger friends. In this case, *longer* exercise periods, not *harder*, are the answer. And if at any time during your workout you become too winded to carry on a normal conversation, you are working too hard; this is your cue to slow down.

So please remember: *know* your own body before you begin, and always in the beginning *easy does it.*

The Best Exercise

Over the years I've tried all kinds of exercise. I've gone the gamut from jogging to cycling to tennis. I've enjoyed each one. But every one of them has its problems—and its drawbacks.

When I discovered rebounding, I felt as if I were in a new world! I hadn't dreamed there was an exercise that could be so enjoyable and so effective at the same time! **All forms of exercise can be beneficial, but rebound exercise offers more benefits than any other form.** Let me give you a few reasons why:

- Rebounding is *one of the best all-around exercises*. When you rebound, every cell of your body is strengthened. Rather than concentrating on strengthening one particular set of muscles, as many exercise programs do, rebounding strengthens your whole body—no part of it is neglected. Therefore, in an overall sense, rebound exercise is the best. Even if you engage in other forms of exercise or other programs, you'd be smart to include a supplementary rebound program *as well*.

- Rebounding is *more convenient* than just about any other form of exercise. You can do it in your home, in your office—wherever you are—with no special clothing, location, or equipment other than your rebound unit itself.

- A rebounding program on a quality unit is *safer* than most other exercise programs. Think of exercising in the safety and comfort of your own home or patio—no strange people or animals to encounter, no fear of being assaulted after dark. Think of having the assurance that injuries seldom, if ever, happen with proper use of the rebound unit.

- Exercising with a rebound unit is *more flexible and easier* than with any other piece of equipment or program. You can dance on your unit, run on it, just have fun on it! Your imagination is your instructor.

- Rebounding is *less costly* than most exercise programs—and that includes jogging. Look at it this way: by the time you've bought a pair of $40 shoes and a jogging outfit with all the accessories, you may have put out a couple of hundred dollars or even more. And those things won't last forever: you'll have to do it all over again when your present gear wears out. Why not buy a quality rebound unit *once* and be done with it?

This list just begins to explain why a rebound unit is your best exercise bargain. That's what this book is all about. In each section I'll give you more details about the use and enjoyment of your rebound unit—and you'll be on your way to a healthier body and the best attitude about exercise you've ever had. I know—that's what happened to me!

The Biggest Mistake You Can Make with Any Exercise Program

I hope you don't think I've always been a good, consistent exerciser. Before I started using a rebound unit, I was probably as consistently inconsistent as anybody. I had my share of excuses. And when I talked with my friends, they had their share, too! Here are some of the ones I've used or heard. See if any sound just the slightest bit familiar:

- "I just don't have the time."

- "I'm too tired."

- "I don't like doing it by myself."

- "I don't want to go out in the cold in the winter."

- "It's too hot to exercise in the summer."

- "The kids get in my way."

- "My kids/husband laugh at me."

- "I'm too old to start now."

- "None of my friends are doing it."

- "It never seems to do any good."

- "It gives me too much of an appetite and then I overeat."

- "I don't like other people to see me sweat."

- "I'm too shy to run in public."

- "There's no convenient place."
- "It costs money, and I don't have any.
- "I'd rather watch TV."
- "I have too far to go—I'd get discouraged before I even got halfway to my goal."
- "Exercise? Are you kidding? The way my kids keep me running all day, I get all the exercise I need."
- "I'm too sick all the time."
- "It's too hard—too much work."
- "I exercised faithfully for a whole month and no one even noticed."
- "I'm pregnant/just had a new baby."
- "Dieting's all I need to keep my girlish figure."
- "I don't look good in a leotard."
- "I don't know how."
- "What if I hurt myself?"
- "I can't motivate myself."
- "It's *boring*."

Did I hit the mark with any of those? How about just a twinge of recognition?

To my way of thinking, all of these excuses could be boiled down to just a few : self-consciousness ("Any exercise program I can think of involves being where other people can see me and my flabby body"), lack of awareness of the need or benefits of exercise ("Oh, exercise isn't all that important"), fear ("What if I get hurt?" or "No way—there are too many muggers out there!"), or just plain apathy ("So exercise is good for me—who cares?").

But there's hope for all of us, no matter what excuse we like to use. Rebounding gives a happy answer to just about any difficulty we can dream up about exercising. There's no need for self-consciousness with a rebound unit—you can exercise in the privacy of your own living, family, or even bedroom. This privacy also eliminates many of the fears associated with exercise. And rebounding handles the fear of injury—it's almost impossible to get hurt on a rebound unit.

What about those whose excuse is apathy—they just don't care? Or what if they aren't aware of the need? To such people I have only one answer, and I'll put it bluntly: "Wake up, and look around you!" All a person needs to do is turn on the TV, open a magazine, or listen to a radio talk show and he or she will hear all kinds of testimonials and scientific proof on the "good life" a healthy body brings—a good life you'll be missing if you don't regularly exercise.

This is probably the biggest mistake people make with any exercise program: they don't realize what an exciting and rewarding part of life it can be. Take a look at that last excuse I listed: "It's *boring.*" That's the excuse I've heard most often. And I can hardly blame those who use it. After all, most exercise approaches can be very monotonous, tedious, and seem like just plain hard work—and any redeeming qualities are pretty hard to find.

But unless you're *looking* for an excuse—and any old one will do—there are answers to that complaint, and they especially work with rebounding. When you're rebounding, it's not too hard to turn exercising into a game.

How about these ideas for starters:

- Turn on some music with a good beat—exercise to polkas, rock and roll, march music
- Listen to classical music
- Focus your mind on something—think through a problem
- Listen to tapes—music, foreign language, other instruction, inspiration, motivation, information
- Recite poetry
- Memorize poetry or songs you'd like to be able to recall
- Be a visualizer—see yourself in some distant exotic spot

21

running on the seashore, go to a place in your mind that you've always wanted to visit, remember an occasion that was particularly pleasant

- Watch TV
- Listen to the radio
- Listen to the police scanner
- Watch a video tape
- Clown around and act silly—nobody's watching you!
- Sing to yourself or with the music
- Do an old high school cheer
- Pretend you are the Bionic Woman
- Recite your philosophy of life; commit it to memory
- Make a list of the good things about yourself and say them out loud
- Release your playfulness—be a kid again
- Exercise in a group or with friends (this is an old stand-by that is nearly always fail-safe).

Any of these helpful hints can turn exercising into a sport, a game, a joy. But when you're doing it on a rebound unit, the exercising will be fun to begin with! I've found that with or without the above activities, a rebound unit will melt your fears away, turn your self-consciousness into confidence, and show you just what it is that you've been missing!

I can even promise you more sparkle in the eye and roses in the cheeks! Then when friends come up to you with a quizzical look in their eyes and say, "Hey, there's something different about your face!" you can really smile—and know that the BIG pay-off has arrived.

And the next time you hear someone say, "Exercise is *boring,*" *You'll* be the one with the enthusiastic testimonial!

22

Take Off Fat
Where You Want

Now I'm going to get personal: I've always had a figure problem. My dad put it this way: "Honey, you have an hourglass figure. Only trouble is, all the sand is in the bottom."

As I got older and started to fight this problem, I found I never could win. No matter what I tried, my hips were always too big. Even when I was successful at losing the *amount* of weight I needed to lose, it would leave in all the wrong places. The pounds above the waist were always the first to go; the pounds below the waist were always the last. Picture how I ended up, every time: a gaunt face, a skinny neck, a diminished bustline—and big hips! The hourglass syndrome had struck again!

When I did succeed in losing weight from my hips, I was still out of proportion. Talk about discouragement! So I would go off the diet—and where would I gain it back first? You guessed it.

But an amazing thing happened when I found rebounding: the extra inches from my hips were the *first* to go! I was ecstatic! Even more exciting was that my other proportions stayed where they were—which was right where I wanted them! At last I had the kind of hourglass that neither my dad nor anyone else could joke about.

23

The reason for this wonderful phenomenon is very simple: **Rebound exercise diminishes fat deposits, while at the same time it tones and builds muscles.** I wanted to lose fat around the hips and maintain tone elsewhere. And that's exactly what rebounding helped me do.

Can you imagine how I felt? For years and years I'd been struggling with this problem. Now, like a miracle, I suddenly had the solution. I felt better about myself. Before, I'd been a little self-conscious in public, especially when wearing pants and certain dresses. But now I shopped for all kinds of new clothes to go with the new me. I felt terrific!

Rebounding isn't good just for hips. Think of the one place you like least on your body. Maybe it's your bust, or your thighs, or your upper arms. Maybe that place is a little too fat, or somewhat out of proportion. Now think of yourself without that problem—your body is perfectly formed, proportioned like your favorite movie star. What's going to take you from now to then? The best road I know is the rebounding road. As you do the right exercises on the rebound unit, you will become trim where you want to be trim. No more sandy bottom or jutting tummy! Instead, you will be more like you always wanted to be. And don't think others won't notice!

How can rebounding do all this for us? Our bodies require certain nutrients in order to function properly. The cells use these nutrients to produce enzymes, which enable the cells to perform their necessary processes. When the cells are robbed of their proper nutrients, they lose tone, their ability to produce enzymes, and their ability to perform efficiently.

This is why dieters often feel run-down. When calorie intake is cut down, the body has to obtain its necessary nutrients from somewhere, and that somewhere is usually healthy, working tissues first—muscle, for example. In order to burn off excess fat tissues, the body robs nutrients from other tissues, thus making them lose tone and decrease productivity, at the same time fat is being used.

Exercising, along with proper nutrition, attacks fat cells *directly*. Other body tissues are able to maintain their proper nutrient levels and function normally, while the fat is burned off in all the right places.

24

Can you lose fat just through dieting? Absolutely! But only at the expense of other, healthy body tissues. Not to mention your own healthy disposition! *Only through a combination of proper nutrition and consistent exercise* can you lose fat where you need to lose it and keep it where you want it. And only that combination will help you keep your weight loss permanent.

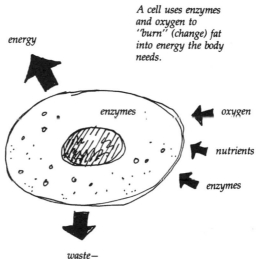

A cell uses enzymes and oxygen to "burn" (change) fat into energy the body needs.

energy

enzymes

oxygen

nutrients

enzymes

waste—
CO_2 and H_2O

How to Get Results with Minimum Effort, Risk, or Injury

You probably know that there are many forms of exercise—all of them beneficial in one way or another. However, when they're stacked up against each other, it quickly becomes evident that rebounding gives better results for toning, conditioning, and general strengthening than anything else you can do—and it does it with less effort, risk, or chance of injury.

Not too long ago a couple of friends of mine, a jogger named Bruce and his wife, Betty, discovered just how effective rebounding really is. Bruce was a confirmed jogger; he'd been running for over three years. Betty also liked to exercise, but pregnancy and a new baby had slowed her down. Then Betty heard about rebounding. Bruce was pretty skeptical when he heard how effective rebounding exercise was supposed to be—but he agreed to go with Betty to check it out.

While the salespeople were giving Betty an explanation of the advantages of the rebound unit, Bruce didn't even listen. Instead, he was actually trying it out. After several minutes of jogging on the rebound unit, Bruce jumped down, came over to them and said enthusiastically, "I'll take one!"

The salespeople were pleased, but surprised. "Great!" they said. "But why? You didn't even hear our presentation."

"It wasn't too hard to decide," Bruce answered. "When I jog, it takes me twenty minutes to get to the right heart rate level for the proper aerobic effect. But this rebound unit gives me that same heart rate in less than half the time! I'm sure it will give us the conditioning results we need *with less effort* than jogging takes."

Compare these forms of exercise with rebounding for efficiency and risk:

- **Isometric exercise** involves contracting a muscle without moving a joint, such as pulling a knob of a locked door, or pushing the palms of your hands or the soles of your feet together. Isometrics work only on the muscles surrounding the bones.

- **Isotonic exercise** involves contracting muscles to produce a range of movements, as in bowling, calisthenics, weight-lifting. Again, you are strengthening skeletal muscles, but your cardiovascular system is being neglected. Isotonic exercise does not demand enough oxygen to have a lasting benefit. And there is always the danger of straining or spraining muscles or joints.

- **Anaerobic exercise** includes stop-and-start sports such as tennis, basketball, racquetball. In playing these games, your body demands large amounts of oxygen, but not for a sufficiently long enough period to be beneficial to heart and lungs. And again, as with an isotonic program, the discomfort of strain or sprain is always possible when using the less conditioned muscles in spurts.

- **Recreational exercise** includes other games such as badminton, croquet, golf, etc., which are engaged in primarily for fun, but do not require the sustained effort needed for lasting cardiovascular benefit.

- **Aerobic exercise** is that form of sustained exercise which, gradually increased over a period of time, strengthens the pulmonary, cardiovascular, lymphatic, muscular, and metabolic systems—all at the same time. In beginning an aerobic program, you have the choice of many activities: rebounding, jogging, swimming, bicycling, etc.

All these are beneficial in an aerobic sense. However, all of these aerobic activities—*except* rebounding—are stressful to the body as well, causing wear and sometimes damage to ankles, knees, hips, spine, shoulders, and other parts of the body.

Look at the problems a runner or jogger can be subject to, for example:

- painful Achilles' tendons
- shin splints
- tight calves or ankles
- torn or tight hamstrings
- lower back or sciatic nerve pain
- foot and arch injuries
- wearing out of foot joints
- lung "burns" in cold weather.

Even though swimming has sometimes been touted as the ultimate exercise, even this favorite has its problems:

- potential eye, ear, nose, throat, and lung infections
- chlorine inhalation
- athlete's foot from public pools
- danger of swimming alone in open water.

Now, take a look at what *rebounding* is like. Being an aerobic exercise, rebounding gives you that excellent workout for cardiopulmonary fitness. In addition, it's the safest exercise program available. With rebounding—

- there's no need to dodge cars, dogs, or snowballs
- no cold air will burn your lungs
- other bad weather hazards will not bother you
- you won't have to search for a place to park or a trail on which to run or cycle
- there is no added exposure to possible rape, robbery, or assault

- your mental concentration won't be distracted by the need to watch for possible dangers

- your weight-bearing joints are spared up to 85 percent of the usual jarring and pounding (on most good-quality units)

- possibility of pulled tendons is minimal

- even pregnant women can safely exercise until the fifth month of pregnancy.

Compare the pros and cons. It doesn't take too much comparing to see that the most pleasant, convenient, and *easy* way to achieve that toned up, conditioned, strengthened body you want is with a quality rebound unit. Think about it: for years you've been wanting the kind of figure that others will compliment you on—or at least notice for its good qualities! There are a lot of ways to reach your goal. But the rebound unit is the best. The *very* best!

How to Get the "Perfect" Figure for You

Let me tell you about Susan T. Her ideal weight is 120 pounds, and that's what she's weighed for the past eight years. Recently she started exercising on a rebound unit for approximately thirty minutes per day. She doesn't want to lose weight, so she eats whatever she wants, within the guidelines of good nutrition. With the approach Susan is taking, she's maintaining her same weight—but something else has happened since she started using the rebound unit: her figure has improved.

Before beginnning a rebounding program, Susan's waist was always thicker than she wanted it to be, and her bustline was smaller. But as she continued her workouts with special exercises on the rebound unit, she noticed that her waistline was decreasing and her bustline was increasing! She has now gained what she considers the perfect figure for her. Her shape is now in shape!

Susan isn't the only one who has come to me with these great results. Another is Melanie: She lost forty pounds in a short period of time with her unit, but she maintains that it wasn't just the loss of weight that has given her a more beautiful figure. At the same time she has *redesigned her curves* in "all the right places" by using the exercises in this book.

Rebound exercise will help you develop a more pleasing figure—the best you can acquire. To find out why this is so, we just need to look under the outer layers we wear.

You see, our muscular and skeletal systems by themselves are normally well-proportioned. When our muscles are well-toned, and we have no fat deposits to ruin the outline, the shape we see on the outside follows nicely along the pattern set for it by the frames we have inside.

Fashion models often have the kind of look I'm talking about. Their *look* starts with their hair and works all the way down to their toes. Their smooth skin follows the outlines of the bone and muscle—you never see fat deposits anywhere in models.

The next time you're around a group of teenage girls, notice their ideal young shapes. Their bodies are young and fresh, filled out with well-toned muscles, and not yet harboring fat deposits.

We don't all have to be models or teenagers—in fact, we don't want to be. But the structure of their bodies shows us what's available with a little effort! Youth doesn't have to be wasted on the young! Rebound exercise, by conditioning and toning your muscles and getting rid of unwanted pounds, can give you the firm, more youthful figure you once had (or wish you had). Or, like Susan, you may not *need* to lose any pounds, but merely redistribute the ones you have. As your muscles become stronger and fat deposits disappear, your body weight will be redistributed. Your beautiful "new" shape will emerge as the pleasing outline that Mother Nature planned for you when she gave you your unique skeletal design.

How to Lose Weight Forever—Without Torturing Yourself

Perhaps the most—well, *inspiring* (I can't think of a better word for it!) story I know about rebounding and losing weight is that of my friend Evelyn B.

She was about fify-five years old, weighed 160 pounds, was 5' 9" and wore a size 16 dress. Unfortunately, along with her weight problem, her husband had left her and her self-image was badly shaken.

Evelyn decided it was time to make a few changes in her life. She bought a rebound unit and started using it, gradually but consistently just jogging and jumping ten minutes a day. Then she began to watch what she ate and cut out junk food.

It wasn't long before I began to notice a change in her appearance. She had started losing weight. Four weeks later she showed me a chart that she had drawn up. "I thought you might be interested in seeing this," she said. The chart showed her losses in pounds and inches, all from her rebounding and dietary improvements.

In just four months' time, Evelyn lost forty pounds and a cumulative total of thirty-and-a-half inches from different parts of her body! Another wonderful thing was happening at the same time: Evelyn's feelings of self-esteem were increasing. Eventually her husband even returned!

MARCH TO START	JUNE	FEBRUARY 1 YR. LATER
WAIST 30"	27½"	24"
HIPS 42¼"	38"	34"
THIGH 23¾"	19"	18"
TUMMY	34"	33"
KNEE 17⅝"	15½"	13½"
CALF 13"	13"	12"
ANKLE 8¾"	8½"	7¾"
ARM 12¼"	11"	8½"

FROM SIZE 16 TO SIZE 8-10
165 lbs. TO 123 lbs. = 42 lbs. LOST
TOTAL INCHES LOST = 30⅜"

Here is a copy of Evelyn's progress chart. She showed improvement in every measurement.

Through simple, consistent exercise, just ten minutes a day, Evelyn was able to lose weight and gain a new self! The last time I saw her she weighed 125 pounds and looked gorgeous and fifteen years younger!

Losing weight can be easy if it is approached properly. Too often we seem to think that losing weight is a super-big deal. But it doesn't have to be. If we'll get on a program that requires at least mild exercise, and start paying attention to our diet, the weight will start to feel unwelcome and will leave!

Why is this so? It all has to do with circulation and cell processes.

When we cut down on our food intake, which is the main form of dieting, we put fewer calories into our bodies. As a result, our bodies have to get energy from somewhere—and the lucky candidates are those calories that are already stored as fat. But that's only part of the story.

It takes more than dieting and using energy to lose fat. In addition, we need to get enough oxygen into the cells to burn off the fat. How does that happen? Simply through having good circulation. How do we get good circulation? Simply by exercising! (You knew I had a moral in here someplace, didn't you!)

Here's why good circulation is so important: Calories don't just burn themselves up. They are burned up by enzymes. The enzymes are formed from nutrients in the food we eat—often in combination with oxygen in the muscles! The enzymes get to the stored fat through the bloodstream. If we have good circulation, the whole process works much more efficiently.

Getting the enzymes to the stored fat is only half the problem, however. In the enzymatic processing of fat cells, waste materials are given off. That's where the circulatory system is needed again—to help remove the waste materials from the cells of the body. Weight loss is the ultimate result.

So there are two approaches here to losing weight: You can torture yourself by watching calories alone and depriving yourself of many of the goodies you like. Or you can just cut down on calories a bit, and then engage in consistent exercise to keep your circulatory system functioning in top-notch condition—and allow your natural bodily processes to do the work of losing weight for you!

Think again of my friend, Evelyn. All she did was jog and jump for ten to fifteen minutes a day, five days a week—and she lost forty pounds in a matter of months. She didn't push hard or overexert; she didn't wear herself out from overdieting or overexercising. She just started a program that fit her needs—and because it was so easy and enjoyable she was able to stick with it.

You can do the same thing! A rebound unit is your ticket to a thinner, healthier figure. You can lose weight forever—without torturing yourself!

How Does Rebound Exercise Work— and Why?

When I first started rebounding—and saw the tremendous results it gave me—I really didn't care how it worked. I just knew it did! But I've since learned what makes rebounding such good exercise, and the explanation makes me even more enthusiastic than I was before.

Every day of our lives, our bodies are subjected to gravitational forces. Those forces are part of our existence. They help to make and shape our bodies.

If we lived in a world where there was no gravity, we wouldn't have any weight. But I believe we'd get incredibly fat—whenever we moved, we wouldn't have the pull of gravity on our bodies. Our actions (the ones we were able to do in weightlessness) wouldn't burn up very many calories.

If we tried to exercise in weightlessness, we'd find it would give us very few benefits. It's the pull of gravity that enables exercise to strengthen our bodies. Gravity is therefore very necessary for proper body functions.

And that brings us to rebounding. **When we rebound, we increase the pull of gravity on our bodies. As a result, the gravitational forces condition, tone, and strengthen each body cell.** The same thing would happen if we just jumped up and down—but that would cause much greater wear and tear on our bodies.

35

Let me use weight-lifting as an example:

The object of weight-lifting is to enlarge the muscles and increase strength. To accomplish this, the weight-lifter raises progressively larger weights, thereby forcing the muscles to tone themselves to a greater degree as they become equal to the greater task. When the weight-lifter increases the amount of weight he's lifting, he's increasing the *gravitational pull* on the cells of his muscles—the larger the weight, the more the gravitational pull. This strengthens the walls of the cells, improves circulation, and produces stronger muscles.

With rebound exercise, this same process takes place in *all* the cells of the body. As you jump on a rebound unit, gravity pulls you down; as you bounce back up, you are *defying* gravity, thereby increasing the gravitational pull on

G-Forces

The more pounds the greater the G-Forces

Rebound exercise strengthens the body by increasing Gravitational Forces (G-Forces). Lifting weights does the same thing. But rebounding is a better overall exercise because it strengthens the whole body not just isolated parts. Also it is a more gentle way to build body strength and improve circulation.

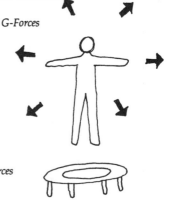

G-Forces

G-Forces

The greater the Acceleration and Deceleration the greater the G-Forces

36

the body. This is the same action you feel when stopping, starting, or turning an automobile: gravitational forces keep pushing or pulling your body in one direction while the vehicle has actually moved in the opposite direction. These same forces affect astronauts because of the speed and pressure they experience when traveling in space capsules.

When you rebound you can increase from the normal pull of one "G-force" on your body to two and even three G-forces. How much extra pressure is this putting on your body? Suppose you weigh 100 pounds. That's the weight the normal pull of gravity (one G-force) gives you. Now you get up on your rebound unit and start to jump; at the lowest point of the bounce, the G-forces can easily double. This means your feet have a weight placed on them of 100 pounds (the normal) plus another 100 pounds (the *extra* G-force), or a total of 200 pounds. The same thing happens with all the cells of your body: the gravitational forces are increased as you begin to move upwards, causing toning and strengthening of each cell.

It's important to note that all bodily functions work with or against gravity. The heart, for example, has to pump the blood against gravity—blood that gravity has pulled to other parts of the body. In swallowing, food is pushed down the esophagus partially by gravity, partially by muscle activity. If there were no gravity to aid the processes of the body, each organ or muscle would have to work at least twice as hard to accomplish its purpose. So it is this constant pushing and pulling against gravity that keeps the body functioning and in shape.

What rebounding accomplishes is to give the body, for short periods of time, extra G-forces to strengthen each and every cell. A simple bounce can result in added benefit; the easy, effortless process of rebounding puts those powerful gravitational forces to work in massaging, strengthening, and improving circulation in each cell of your body.

You've probably noticed the strength and agility of members of gymnastic teams. These athletes continually work with G-forces in the maneuvers and routines that they perfect. The rebound unit will do the same for you; as each cell becomes improved and strengthened, the whole body benefits.

This principle is graphically demonstrated in the effects experienced by astronauts whose bodies were deprived of gravitational forces for long periods of time. When they returned from the weightlessness of outer space, their cells had begun to undergo adjustments to the atmosphere. Where there had been no gravitational pull on the cells, they had experienced very little stress, and therefore became weaker. Measurements of the astronauts' bodies indicated that they had actually *lost* 15 percent of their bone density!

As you can see, not only *should* we make use of the G-forces to tone our bodies, we *need* them in order to function at our optimum level here on the earth.

Try it for yourself: Bounce a few times on your rebound unit and concentrate on the sensations produced by the G-forces on your body. As you reach the bottom of each bounce, you will actually feel the tugging of gravity on your face, your shoulders, and so forth; then, as you reach the apex of the bounce, you will feel a moment of weightless floating before you descend again. You can actually feel each cell being compressed and expanded—massaged—for strengthening and conditioning. You are getting the results of good, quality exercise with very little effort on your part. Gravity, because of the rebounding process, is doing most of the work for you.

Remember the fun you had as a child jumping on your parents' bed? The feeling of lightness alternating with the exhilarating feeling of being pushed back up again as you hit those springs? If someone had told you then that you were massaging and strengthening your body cells you would have laughed at them. "I'm just having fun!" Well, why not be a child again? Have your exercise and enjoy it too!

Rebounding Cleans the Cells

I received a most exciting phone call one day. A friend of mine called to tell me of an amazing "healing" experience he'd had because of his rebound exercise. He explained that he had come down with a bad cold, had become very ill with it, and didn't seem to be able to shake it. Then one morning he decided to exercise on his rebound unit anyway. He went through a rather vigorous session, and, to his surprise, he felt much better because of it. Even more to his surprise, as he continued to exercise, his cold went away; and before the day was over, he was completely rid of it.

Some time after this, my husband began to come down with the flu. He awoke in the morning feeling sluggish and achy. Remembering what our friend had told us, my husband decided to try this "cure" for himself. He normally exercises with the rebound unit from twelve to twenty minutes a day. This day he decided to exercise twenty extra minutes, and at a very vigorous pace. He really didn't feel like exercising at all, let alone for an extra twenty minutes. But he was glad he did, because he never really did come down with the flu that was going around. The symptoms left him, and he felt great.

Rebounding seems to clean toxins and poisons from

individual cells by stimulating the cells and increasing circulation of body fluids to them.

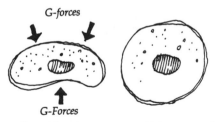

Gravitational forces alternately put pressure on and take pressure off body cells thereby massaging and stimulating the cells. Rebounding also improves circulation to aid the body's fight against disease. Better circulation helps cleanse the cells by eliminating waste and harmful toxins.

Picture each cell as a sponge. Suppose that sponge is full of dirty water. When you squeeze the sponge you flush the dirty water out. Then you put the sponge in fresh, clean water and allow it to soak in.

Rebounding allows gravity forces to squeeze bacteria and toxins out of the cells, and to be flushed out by normal bodily processes, just as the dirty water was squeezed out of the sponge.

Try this for yourself the next time you feel you're beginning to catch a cold. Rather than eliminate exercise, as we are apt to do because we don't feel well, continue your rebound program daily to allow your cells to be cleaned of harmful substances and strengthened against the disease. Don't overdo, of course, to the point of *weakening* your body and wearing yourself down. But give your cells a good workout to enable your body to cure itself. You'll be amazed at how much better you feel!

By the way, a consistent, daily exercise program will eliminate much of the sickness you otherwise may be susceptible to, and your tendency to catch every little thing that comes along will be greatly decreased. Remember the old adage, "An apple a day keeps the doctor away"? The same thing applies to exercise. Using your rebound unit every day can keep the medical bills away!

A Beginning Program

One of the comments I hear over and over about rebounding is "Now wait a minute—this is so *easy*. Just jumping up and down—something this easy can't really be doing that much good!" They belong to the "sweat and ache" school of thought—they've been convinced that you have to absolutely wear yourself out for an exercise to be of any benefit. If you don't "sweat and ache," in fact, if the exercise is *fun*, how can it possibly give beneficial results?

Our society seems to have been trained in the Puritan ethic: you have to work for what you get. And work hard! But exercise is one area where that old truism doesn't necessarily hold true. Especially if you do it right.

What most people don't realize is that rebounding is good exercise, and better exercise than most programs *because* of its simplicity. With only one kind of motion, the rebound unit tones and conditions every single cell of the body at once. Thus rebounding is what you might call a concentrated form of exercise—you actually get more results from less effort. (See "How does Rebound Exercise Work—and Why?")

Yes, rebounding is easy. So why not relax and enjoy it? *Let* it be easy. Take advantage of its simplicity and don't waste energy trying to complicate it.

I'm going to use something we all understand for an example—laundry detergent. There are many brands on the market these days that boast of being a "concentrated" product. Their television ads will profess over and over that all it takes is "that little quarter cup" to make a full load of dirty, grimy work clothes "cleaner than clean."

If you're like me, you've seen those ads and have been just a little bit skeptical of their claims. I have one friend who decided the manufacturers must be exaggerating, and she used three times as much detergent as was recommended, "just to be sure." You can imagine what she ended up with: A clogged-up washing machine, "suds in the closet" from the excess solution not being rinsed out of the clothes, and a definitely too-soon-empty container of detergent.

The same thing applies to rebounding. There's no good reason to use more than you need. Even if you *think* you're not getting enough. As the motto of another kind of concentrated product used to say, "A little dab'll do ya."

Let me show you just how concentrated rebounding can be. I have an acquaintance, named Philip, who gets his exercise in small doses—and finds it's all he needs. Phil is fifty years old, is slender and in good shape, and has a resting heart rate of 50 beats per minute—surprisingly low for anyone (the normal is between 70-80), but perhaps especially for someone his age. Phil maintains his excellent body condition with a rebounding program of approximately fifteen minutes per day, which, incidentally, is a somewhat *advanced* program. Phil is in good enough condition to continue past that initial fifteen minutes, but why should he when this is all he needs to keep in such great shape. His philosophy is, "Rebounding is so easy—why make it hard?"

If you are amazed that he can get by on only fifteen minutes a day, you'll be *thrilled* to learn what a beginning program entails. We start out slowly and work up very gradually—you won't think it's work at all. But while you're doing all that "non-work," you'll be getting yourself into shape!

The Beginning Program

First day: Start very slowly, bouncing with both feet *maintaining contact* with the rebound unit at all times (do not allow your feet to rise above the mat), for *one minute.* Repeat at least twice a day, once in the morning and once in the evening, and up to five times a day if you're able. (Note: Do not rebound for five consecutive minutes. The conditioning results will occur more effectively if the exercise periods do not exceed one minute each time).

Second day: Repeat the above exercise for *one-and-a-half minutes,* at least twice a day, and up to five times a day if you're able.

Third day: Repeat the above exercise, this time allowing your feet to leave the rebound unit occasionally, for the same amount of time. In addition, *walk* on the rebound unit for one minute. Repeat these two actions at least twice a day, and up to five times a day if you're able.

Fourth day: Bounce, again for one-and-a-half minutes, and walk from *two to five* minutes, *twice* during the day.

Fifth day: Bounce one-and-a-half minutes, then *walk and jog* on the rebound unit for two to five minutes, twice during the day.

Sixth day: Bounce one-and-a-half minutes, then jog a little more strenuously than before for *five minutes,* twice during the day, bringing your knees a little higher than before.

Seventh day: Now we begin a longer, once-a-day program. First, bounce for one-and-a-half minutes, then jog for *six minutes,* and finally *cool down for one minute* by walking on the unit.

From this point, your object is to work up to a total exercise time of twelve minutes per day. You should begin each session with a warm-up of bouncing for about a minute, and end each session with a cool-down of about a minute. The jogging time in between should be gradually increased until the total rebounding time is about ten minutes. The program is made more strenuous by jogging harder or raising the legs higher, but again, *the total time should not exceed twelve minutes for a beginning program.*

A Note about Clothing

When you are rebounding, you can wear just about anything you want. Since you're in the privacy of your own home, you can wear a bathrobe or a bikini, whichever works best. Most people find they can wear their everyday clothes, though some prefer sweat pants or gym shorts.

There is one thing women should keep in mind when they're deciding what to wear when using their rebound unit: a proper fitting bra with good support is an essential part of their dress. I've found that over 30 percent of the women who exercise are not properly "rigged"—and the result is soreness, chafing, and discomfort from the constant and uncontrolled movements of the breasts.

So when you're jumping and jogging, dress as you please—but, ladies, be sure your *underdress* is right!

The best way to get started on a rebounding program is to walk in place on the unit.

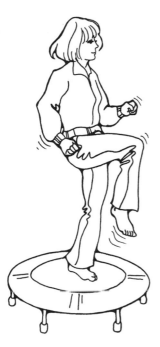

The basic exercise of the beginning program is the Low Jog. The low jog involves lifting the feet off the mat but not raising the knees too high.

Another basic movement is the Jump Rope. Simply perform the movements of jumping rope, either with or without the rope!

Are You Ready for an Advanced Rebound Program?

Once you have prepared your body adequately through the beginning program, you are ready to start an advanced exercise routine. Your stamina is now well-established and your muscles and other tissues are well-conditioned, and you feel generally in good shape.

Basically, an advanced rebound program is an extension of the beginning routine. You just continue doing the same things *for a longer period of time.* The advanced program isn't harder, just longer. You may want to begin to *vary* the different kinds of movements that you do on the rebound unit—but that's totally optional. The program will vary from person to person—what is an advanced program for you may be completely different from what someone else chooses to do. It need not be more strenuous, unless *you* want it to be. The only real requirement for an advanced rebound program is that it be *longer* than the beginning exercise.

So all I have to say about the "rules" of an advanced program are these few *do*s and *don'ts*:

DON'T—

• go too far too fast. Just as you did with the beginning

program, work up to your maximum time slowly, gradually increasing the amount of time from day to day.

- expect it to be hard. An advanced rebound program has all the same things you loved about it in the beginning: it's convenient, effective, and *easy*.

- expect it to hurt. Just go slow and easy, as you've always done before. Add only thirty seconds or a minute a day. Let those muscles get used to the extra exercise gradually—sneak up on them and they'll never know the difference!

DO—

- take it easy. Again, a little at a time is sufficient. And most people find that even with an advanced program, fifteen to thirty minutes a day is just plenty; fifteen minutes is the minimum, thirty the maximum for most people. And that's a snap!

- have fun! There's no reason to be bored with a rebound unit. Dance, jump, do *your* thing. And if "your thing" happens to be straight, even jogging—do it and enjoy!

- set a regular daily routine. In order to get the greatest amount of effectiveness from any exercise routine, it needs to be a regular thing. One day this week, four days next, two the following week, and back to one after that just won't do it. It doesn't have to be every day, but every other day, and preferably four days a week is highly recommended.

- include your own specialized exercises. While rebounding is an excellent program for all-over toning and conditioning, there are specific exercises for trimming hips, building stamina, etc. (A look at the various sections of this book will help you see what kinds of specific exercises you can do.) Use these as much and as often as you desire. Or as little!

You think you're ready, then, for an advanced rebound program? It's all yours—take it away!

EXERCISE	DAY	MONDAY	TUESDAY	WEDNESDAY	THURSDAY	FRIDAY	SATURDAY	SUNDAY
WARM UP & STRETCH		5	5	5	5	5	5	X
LOW JOG		10	10	10	10	10	10	X
ARM CIRCLES		5	5	5	5	5	5	X
SITTING BOUNCE		5	5	5	5	5	5	X
SIDE KICK		5	5	5	5	5	5	X
HIP TWIST		5		5		5		X
JUMP ROPE			5		5		5	X
TOTAL		30	30	30	30	30	30	X

It's usually helpful to make a chart to show your exercise program. Note that some exercises can be done simultaneously, such as the Low Jog and the Arm Circles. You may also want to alternate exercises on different days of the week, such as the Hip Twist and the Jump Rope.

EXERCISE	DAY	MONDAY	TUESDAY	WEDNESDAY	THURSDAY	FRIDAY	SATURDAY	SUNDAY

The jumping rope movements have a good place in the advanced program.

The key to the advanced program is to increase the length of time you exercise. In addition, you may, if you wish, jog faster and lift your legs higher.

Stretch

Have you ever watched an extremely elderly person walk? One word can usually be used to describe their way of moving: "shuffling." Such older people are hunched over, take short steps, and breathe in short, panting puffs.

Much of the reason for this is that most older people are not very elastic. They must take those short breaths because their chest muscles won't stretch and allow them good, deep breaths. They shuffle because they can't get their legs to stretch as far as they used to. And they hunch because those muscles have become so stiffened that straightening is difficult, if not impossible.

Those of us in our "younger" years need to take this as a definite forewarning. How important it is that we s-t-r-e-t-c-h our muscles every single day! We need to keep our bodies limber and supple and able to reach and do the things we ask them to do. Just as an animal will stretch and yawn and pull every muscle upon waking from a nap, so must we follow the same process to get ourselves going.

But don't try to do stretching to warm up! According to physiologist Dr. John Greenleaf, who developed key physical fitness routines for the astronauts, you don't warm up by stretching. Such exercises should always be preceded by jumping jacks or running. Stretching can pull or strain a cold muscle. For instance, touching the toes while keeping the knees straight "forces your back to stretch beyond its normal range of montion, and that can seriously hurt back muscles," according to Dr. Greenleaf. So, when it's time to warm up, try a low jog, some gentle jumping jacks, or simply jump gently on your rebound unit for a few minutes. Do your stretching *after* your muscles are warmed up.

You are probably aware that most gymnasts, dancers, and athletes go through a systematic progression of stretch-type routines before beginning their regular workouts. This prevents the tearing of vital muscles when they are used in aggressive, fast actions such as running, jumping, or leaping. The key words are these: *systematic progression.* They start small and easy, then work up.

Don't fail to warm up as you start your rebound exercise each day. And don't hesitate to stretch—it's good for you! It can make a lot of difference. You might even prefer stretching after you have completed your rebound exercise routine. That's the way I enjoy doing it and it sure feels good to have a full range of motion without the strain that is felt when muscles are cold.

What To Do on Those Hectic Days When You Don't Have Time to Exercise?

We've all had days like the one I had last week. It's called biting off more than you can chew, planning more than you have time for, having your fingers in too many pies. You know how it goes:

My alarm didn't go off when it was supposed to, so I was late starting. My daughter couldn't find her shoes and I had to make a frantic dash around the house right when I should have been driving her and the other children to school. When I got back I had barely enough time to get the bread dough going before starting the cookie recipe that I'd promised to have done and delivered to the Halloween party at school by noon. Between putting cookie sheets in the oven, taking them out, removing cookies to the cooling rack, and icing the cooled ones, I managed to get in a load of laundry (including my husband's last decent white shirt that he just *had* to have for a meeting that night). In the meantime, my new neighbor from next door came over to ask a few questions about the nearest supermarket, doctor's office, laundromat, etc. I was so busy being nice to her that my bread dough rose higher than it should have and I had to punch it down and start it all over again.

I managed to get the cookies to the school on time, but the afternoon wasn't any better than the morning had been. I had an appointment to get my hair done at two o'clock but the bread wasn't on schedule, so I had to wait to take it out of the oven before I could leave. While I was waiting, I finished typing the last chapter of the thesis I had contracted to do for a university student, which he was going to pick up just before I had to leave for a voice lesson at 5:30. Since I was a few minutes late to my hair appointment, I was out an *hour* later than expected, and still had to pick up the kids at school and fix dinner before I could get ready for the aforementioned lesson. I was doing just great, though, and had accomplished all those things with—miraculously—still enough time for my daily twenty minutes to unwind on the rebound unit before showering and getting ready to leave. Suddenly I remembered my husband's white shirt, which, although permanent press, had sat in the dryer all day and would surely be wrinkled by now. No problem, I thought. All I have to do is whirl it through another few times and the wrinkles will be gone. But when I went to turn on the machine, I discovered that it *wouldn't* move, let alone whirl—the belt was broken.

Now desperate, I whipped out the ironing board and iron and did what I hoped would be a passable job—then looked at the clock.

There went the exercise time! I now had only half an hour left before I had to go, and it takes me exactly twenty-five minutes to shower, dress, and put on my makeup.

What should I do? I'll tell you what I did: even though I had only five minutes to spare, I used them for exercise. I warmed up for about 20 seconds and then used the rest of the five minutes for a short, but very useful jog on my unit.

If you think *that* day was hectic, you ought to hear about the day one of my friends had that same week. She works full time out of the home, and that more than doubles the things she has to worry about.

On this particular day, she got up at 6:00 a.m. to get ready for work, left the house at 7:00 a.m to commute to work and arrived at eight. All day long it was hassle, hassle, hassle, and pressure, pressure, pressure. She had so many problems that she didn't even have time for lunch. At 5:00 p.m., work was over—but then she had to rush to another building for a monthly sales meeting. It was over at 6:30.

Back she went to her car for the hour trip home. At 7:30 she pulled into her driveway and ran into the house to fix supper for a hungry brood. (Her husband was on an out-of-town business trip.) Supper was at 8. She cleaned up the kitchen and the rest of the house for the next hour and put the children in bed. Then it was 9:30. She called her eight-year-old's Cub Scout den mother to coordinate on an activity. At 9:45 it was time to take a warm shower and read in bed for a few minutes before falling asleep. She was too exhausted to exercise.

But she decided she would anyway. "Even when I'm too tired to move, I try to do my rebounding," she told me later. "I might wonder if I have the energy even to walk on it, but after ten minutes of jogging I feel like a new woman. It really makes a difference."

(I've learned she made the right choice. A soccer coach and sports trainer explained how it works. He told me that a person should *never* go to bed exhausted—if she does, she'll find her sleep isn't relaxed or beneficial. No matter how tired we are, we should get up on the rebound unit and simply relax every muscle in our bodies gently for a few moments. Then we'll really rest well, and our bodies and minds will be refreshed and alert in the morning.)

One of the most common excuses people use for *not* exercising is that they don't have the time. And maybe they really don't. But that's if they aren't rebounding. Since rebounding is concentrated exercise, you *can* do it for only a very short period of time and still get excellent results.

In addition, with rebounding you don't *lose* time driving or walking to and from your place of exercise, or changing clothes. Your rebound unit is always there, always convenient, always ready when you're ready.

It is vitally important to be *consistent* in an exercise program; consistency is perhaps *the* most important factor. If you can't exercise every day, do it at least every *other* day. And if *today* is an exercise day, don't skip it, no matter what. With a rebound unit you don't have to. Even five minutes will give you a new lease on your day!

And if by chance you have "one of those days" every now

and then when you can devote only five minutes instead of your regular twenty or thirty, go ahead and spend only five minutes. Then simply add a few minutes to your workouts on the following days of that week. A little exercise on a rebound unit is better than none—and it can make all the difference in how you feel!

Slimming Hips

I mentioned in another section my problem with my "hourglass figure" (my father always said, "All the sand is in the bottom."). Whenever I tried to lose weight, it always came off my face, arms, and bust first—and my hips last—so I ended up with the same out-of-proportion shape I'd started with. Imagine my before-and-after pictures: *Before*—big hips, small face, arms, and bust. *After*—big hips, smaller face, arms and bust.

It was almost enough to make me want to give up and go on a lifelong eating binge!

Then I discovered the secrets of rebounding! At last I had a way to lose weight *from my hips*—where I needed and wanted to lose it—and keep the other proportions of my figure just the way they should be.

I'm not the only one who was blessed with such a wonderful-type figure! I've known a good number of other women who have lost considerable amounts of weight from their hips, while keeping the rest of their bodies the way they wanted them to be. And the same thing can happen for you as well.

Why does rebounding work on the hips? Women have a layer of what is called "subcutaneous fat," which lies right underneath their skin. This layer is simply a collection of fat deposits—and the most vulnerable spot seems to be the hip area. When we women rebound, these fat deposits are attacked directly by the exercise action and are burned away while our muscles are being toned and conditioned.

In addition to your exercise program, be sure to decrease your calorie intake to only those that are necessary. You want to burn off "old" calories (those fat deposits), and stop collecting the new ones you take in. It's only when the enzymes don't get enough new calories to feed on that they can begin to burn the "stored" ones.

As for the rebounding itself, when you are concentrating on one area of your body (the hips, for instance), all you really need to do is jog for longer periods of time until you lose the inches you want to lose, and then cut back again to your normal maintenance routine. For example, if you are not losing the extra amount that you desire with a twenty-minutes-daily program, increase your rebound time to thirty minutes a day, or forty-five, even up to an hour each day for a month, if that's what it takes to get that weight off. It's longer, not harder, exercise you need. (You can break that thirty minutes or an hour a day into two exercise periods, if you like.)

When you have reached your goal, drop back to your original twenty or thirty minutes a day to *keep* those fatty deposits off. Whether you exercise for twenty minutes or thirty depends on you. This is totally an individual thing: It may take you longer to get the weight off than it does your friend down the street. It may take you a longer daily maintenance program to keep it off. Find out what works for you. (The nice thing about rebounding is that once you have reached your goal of weight loss, you should be able to go back to eating about what you want—within reason—and still maintain your ideal measurement *if you maintain a good exercise program.)*

This—the longer daily jog—is all that is needed to get results in one particular area of your body. But if you are engaged in an advanced program and would like a little variation, have some fun with the Hip Twist:

Begin to jog lightly on your rebound unit; jump low and get your rhythm going. Then bend one knee, and bring it up and across your body, then down again. Repeat this motion several times and then repeat it with the other knee. (This exercise is also excellent for stomach muscles and for low back pain.)

Another advanced exercise is the Flutter Kick. It's just what it sounds like—the same thing you do in swimming. Lie face down on the unit with your arms folded under your chin, your trunk across the width of the rebound unit, and your legs outstretched behind you off the unit. Now, keeping your legs straight, kick them alternately up and down, toes pointed, hips tucked under, as quickly as you can. (Be careful not to smash your toes on the floor!)

Now just because I call this an "advanced" exercise, don't get the idea that it has to be *harder* than the normal jogging, that it should take more out of you. That simply isn't true. The only reason I call it advanced is that it is *not* jogging (see Beginning and Advanced Program sections).

You can do this Flutter Kick on the floor, of course, but doing it on the rebound unit just makes it easier for you to execute: your body is cushioned by the flexible mat of the unit, you have something to hold onto with your hands, and you can kick higher when you are off the ground a few inches.

Do these exercises work? Consider my new before and after pictures: *Before*—big hips, small face and arms and bust. *After*—smaller hips and smaller face and arms and bust.

My *new*, truly hourglass figure (no sand in bottom) proves the rebound unit does just what's needed for hips! And I feel terrific!

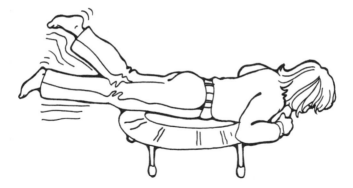

To do the Flutter Kick, lie face down on
the unit and kick the legs up and down.

The Hip Twist is excellent for slimming
hips. While jogging lightly on the
rebound unit, bend one knee and bring it
up in front of you, then return it to the
mat. Do the same with the other knee,
and continue with the alternating motion.

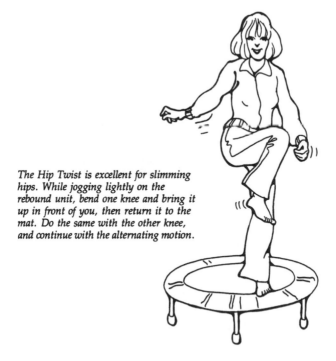

The Fling is a useful exercise for slimming hips. Bring one leg up, bend the knee, and point the toe inward toward the other knee. Repeat with the other leg.

The Sitting Bounce is good for both tummy and hips. Sit in the middle of the rebound unit and bounce up and down, using your arms and legs to lift you off the mat. As your muscles become stronger, keep your legs off the floor and use your arms to do the work.

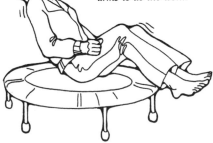

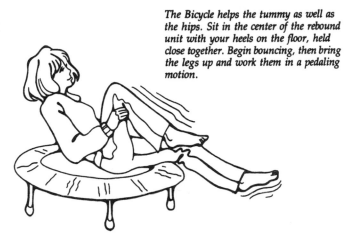

The Bicycle helps the tummy as well as the hips. Sit in the center of the rebound unit with your heels on the floor, held close together. Begin bouncing, then bring the legs up and work them in a pedaling motion.

The Low Jog, simply jogging on the mat, is good for all body toning and trimming needs, including the hips.

The Jump Rope is excellent for hips. The motion is the same whether you use a real rope or an imaginary one.

Firming the Stomach

How's your profile, ladies? And I don't mean your face. Are control-top panty hose your normal wear? Is a girdle a necessity? Would you like to do something about it?

Most of us would enjoy having a nice, flat tummy. It certainly makes us look better in slacks, skirts, and just about anything else. It makes us feel younger, and more confident in our appearance. Nothing's worse than wishing you didn't have that extra tube around your middle—and being unable to get rid of it.

But having well-conditioned stomach muscles includes a much greater benefit than just looking good. This band of muscles holds all of our internal organs in place. When the stomach muscles are well-toned we feel better *inside* as well as outside because our "innards" are where they are supposed to be and can function better.

There's another thing stomach muscles do. Our stomach muscles and some of our back muscles work together, and when they are out of shape we usually start to suffer from lower back pains. When these abdominal muscles are in good condition our backs can handle more stress without discomfort; and when abdominal muscles are strengthened, many back problems are solved.

Are you tired of walking around with an aching back? Tired of feeling "loose" and uncontrolled in the middle? Tired of

63

not having the slender mid-section profile you've always wanted? Don't give up! Your goal is in sight!

There are several ways you can use rebounding to strengthen your stomach muscles. The first way is to use the simple jog that you've been doing all along. The simple motion of raising your legs in the jogging action uses abdominal muscles—and that automatically strengthens them. While you are jogging you can actually feel those internal organs moving around and responding to the gravitational forces placed upon them; they *need* to be held in place. So the jogging *creates* a need for those stomach muscles to be strengthened and then *answers* that need by toning and conditioning the muscles.

To carry this motion farther, try lifting your knees *higher* as you jog. This causes the abdominals to work even harder and concentrates the strengthening power where it is needed most.

An *advanced* exercise that is beneficial to this area is the Front Kick: While jumping slowly on your rebound unit, kick one foot at a time straight out in front of you. A caution with this one: it is easy to lose your balance, so begin with *low* kicks. Then, when you feel confident in your balance, kick a little higher. The higher, the better—but be careful.

Another very good advanced exercise is one you may have tried on the floor (exercise programs are very big on this one). Do you remember the V-Sit? This is the one where you sit on the floor, lift your legs straight up in front of you, raise your arms out to the sides, and try (notice I say "try"!) to balance on your derriere. This takes a great deal of control from your stomach muscles—you can really *feel* them working.

With the rebound unit, you can carry the good effects even farther. Sit on the rebound unit, get yourself in the V-Sit position with legs up and arms out, and then rock back and forth from one hip to the other. Yes, it's a killer, but oh, so good for you!

For some reason, women find this exercise more difficult than men do. It has something to do with the way we're put together, but I think the main problem is one of balance. *If* you can get balanced just right on your buttocks (this is where doing it on the rebound unit is nice, because then you don't feel that hard floor right underneath your tailbone) *and* if you are really concentrating on keeping those stomach muscles as tight as you can, you can do it. And it will really bring the results you want.

A third stomach-strengthener is the Leg Lift. This one is simple, but very beneficial as well. Sit on the edge of the unit with your legs straight out in front of you. Firmly grip the side of the unit. Rest your heels on the floor, then raise both legs together—just a few inches—until they are parallel to the floor. Lower the legs, then repeat. This is good for the thighs as well as the stomach.

The Leg Lift is another exercise that is usually done on the floor but that works even better when done on a rebound unit. When you sit on the unit and force your legs to go down to a level below the rest of your body, you are giving your abdominals an extra stretch and an opportunity to work that they don't get when you do the exercise on the floor.

A final exercise that I like for strengthening the stomach muscles is the Bicycle. Sit in the center of the rebound unit with your heels touching the floor and held close together. Begin bouncing rhythmically, then raise your legs and begin a pedaling motion as if you were riding a bike. This calls for strength from your stomach to begin with, but you will notice an increase in your strength and ability to perform this exercise as you continue doing it.

The Sitting Bounce is good for both tummy and hips. Sit in the middle of the rebound unit and bounce up and down, using your arms and legs to lift you off the mat. As your muscles become stronger, keep your legs off the floor and use your arms to do the work.

The Front Kick is a good advanced exercise. While jumping slowly on the rebound unit, kick one foot out in front of you. Repeat with the other foot. Start with low kicks and work up.

66

The Low Jog, simply jogging on the mat, is good for all body toning and trimming needs. The tummy is no exception.

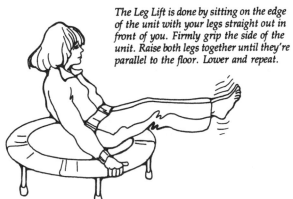

The Leg Lift is done by sitting on the edge of the unit with your legs straight out in front of you. Firmly grip the side of the unit. Raise both legs together until they're parallel to the floor. Lower and repeat.

The Bicycle helps the tummy as well as the hips. Sit in the center of the rebound unit with your heels on the floor, held close together. Begin bouncing, then bring the legs up and work them in a pedaling motion.

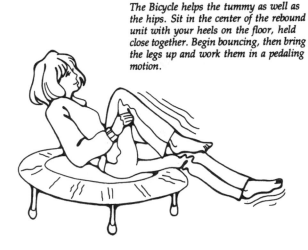

To do the V-Sit, sit on the rebound unit, put your legs up and arms out to the sides, and rock back and forth from one hip to the other.

68

Conditioning Legs

A beautiful leg can certainly turn heads! But even the nicest leg can have hidden problems. And if the leg isn't so beautiful to start with—well, all of us know personally or through friends the agony of varicose veins, leg pains, excess fat, and so forth.

In other sections of this book I talk more about those problems, dealing with them in detail. In the meantime, take a good look at these ideas, because I'm going to tell you here about prevention: if the legs are kept in good condition to begin with, many of the other problems will not occur. At the same time, conditioning the legs will help greatly to resolve problems that do exist.

For example, Kate was head nurse in a large nursing home. She had been plagued with leg pain for several years. But her pains disappeared when she started exercising on a quality rebound unit.

Then her husband was hospitalized; he had suffered complications following open-heart surgery. The hospitalization, combined with Kate's work schedule, wouldn't permit her to use her rebound unit regularly—and she noticed a return of her leg pains.

After her husband returned home from the hospital, Kate returned to her daily 5:00 a.m. workout on the rebound unit—and the pains again went away.

Kate is not an isolated example. I know quite a number of people whose leg difficulties have been helped by rebounding. And who knows how many have been helped by preventive rebounding?

It's not difficult to condition the legs. It really takes nothing more than the usual jog. If you are having problems with your legs, gradually increase the time of your daily jog until you see results.

Some people want to move on to more advanced exercises, however. One good one is the Side Jump:

With your feet together, stand on the right side of the rebound unit. Begin to bounce gently, then bounce across sideways, with both feet landing together on the left side of the rebound unit. Continue doing this, back and forth, back and forth, with your knees and hips slightly bent. Be sure to face straight ahead and keep your trunk still so that the action takes place below the hips only. Practice this exercise daily; before long you'll know how it feels to be a champion slalom ski racer! (It's important that you have a quality rebound unit with six legs, so it doesn't tip over.)

Here's another exercise you may want to try, simply for the sake of variety:

Lie face down on the rebound unit, with your trunk across its width, your elbows resting on the floor, and your legs extended behind you. Alternately raise one foot, then the other, toward your buttocks. Repeat slowly for several minutes. That's all there is to it! But it really can help!

Since our legs are what carry us through our daily tasks, it might be said that they are our power source. So whatever you can do to charge up and condition that source will mean more overall energy for you in the long run. Take good care of your legs and they'll take good care of you.

The Side Kick is good for both legs and thighs. Jog slowly until you have a good rhythm going. Then alternately raise one leg, then the other, kicking out to the side each time.

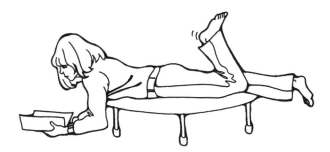

To do the Foot Raise, lie face down on the rebound unit, with your trunk across its width, your elbows resting on the floor, and your legs extended behind you. Alternately raise one foot, then the other, toward your buttocks.

71

The Low Jog, simply jogging on the mat, is good for all body toning and trimming needs, including the legs.

The Leg Lift, which is excellent for conditioning legs, is done by sitting on the edge of the unit with your legs straight out in front of you. Firmly grip the side of the unit. Raise both legs together until they're parallel to the floor. Lower and repeat.

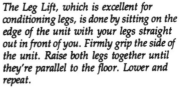

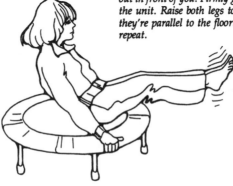

The Knee Walk is another good leg conditioner. The exercise is performed by kneeling on the mat and walking in place on your knees.

The Bicycle is a good leg exercise. Sit in the center of the rebound unit with your heels on the floor, held close together. Begin bouncing, then bring the legs up and work them in a pedaling motion.

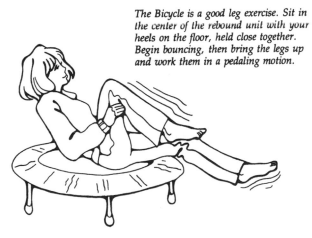

The Jump Rope is excellent for legs. The motion is the same whether you use a real or an imaginary rope.

The Side Jump is done by placing your feet together and standing on one side of the rebound unit. Begin to bounce gently, then bounce across sideways, with both feet landing together on the opposite side of the unit.

A Better Bustline

Why is it that few women seem to be satisfied with their bustline? We are uncomfortable with its largeness or its smallness, its shape or its outline, the sagginess or the fullness—it seems that we always want to improve it in some way.

Whether that's good or not-so-good doesn't matter. Now we have an answer:

Rebound exercise works in different ways to help different women to improve their bustlines.

My problem was that whenever I went on a weight-losing campaign, the first pounds to go would be from my bust—and I wanted to lose from my hips! As far as I was concerned, my bustline was just fine. My problem was preserving it.

When I began rebounding, I found to my great delight that the weight loss *was from my hips,* which had responded to the special exercises for them, and my bustline stayed in its proper proportion so I had a better figure. I was pleased, to say the least! (An unexpected plus was the firming and reduction in size of my upper arms.)

Yvonne D. is another example. She thought her bustline sagged—and she says that rebounding has solved that problem: her bustline has been raised two inches. This came from no special exercises, only the basic gentle jog and bounce that happens to be good for every area of the body.

Debbie R. was too heavy; the weight loss she has received from using the rebound unit has given her a better proportioned body in all areas. She is losing the overhanging rolls and blubbery bulges that gave her figure such an unattractive outline; her improved silhouette is very pleasing, even though she's only used her unit about two months.

What do I recommend for you?

First of all, in any exercise program, you must wear the right "uniform," which includes a good, supporting bra. I cannot emphasize too much how important this is.

Secondly, try just the simple, basic rebound routine: a gentle bounce and jog. This really should be all you need. The rebound action works on all parts of your body, applying whatever is needed wherever it is needed.

Next, add some arm movements if you desire. Rotate your extended arms in small circles while jogging or bouncing on the unit; you will be able to feel all kinds of muscle movement and usage throughout your shoulder area. This strengthens the chest muscles, which of course are the ones that affect your bustline.

Or try holding your arms straight out in front of you or as far and as high behind you as you can while you jog or bounce. Hold the position for as long as you can.

Are you skeptical about the idea of rebound exercise being able to improve your bustline? Think of it in these terms: rebounding tones, firms, and conditions each muscle. When the muscles are strengthened, the surrounding tissues have a better form, a better outline. This is what our bustlines consist of—tissues supported and shaped by underlying muscles. It's just like any other problem: you take care of what's underneath it all, and then everything else just seems to automatically improve.

The Low Jog, simply jogging on the mat, is good for all body toning and trimming needs. The bustline is no exception.

The Jump Rope is a good exercise for the bustline. The motion is the same whether you use a real or an imaginary rope.

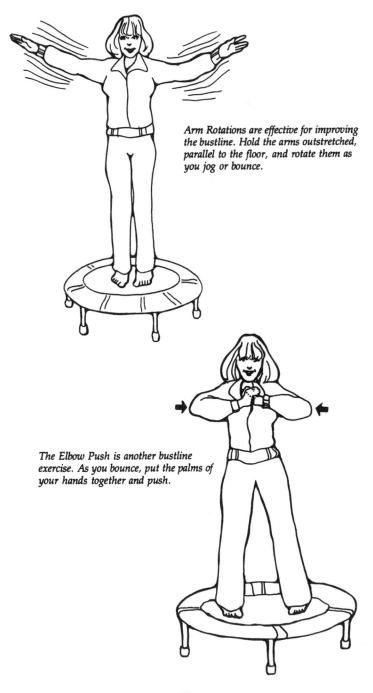

Arm Rotations are effective for improving the bustline. Hold the arms outstretched, parallel to the floor, and rotate them as you jog or bounce.

The Elbow Push is another bustline exercise. As you bounce, put the palms of your hands together and push.

Slimming Thighs

Have you ever wondered how all those beauty pageant contenders get into such great shape and have such confidence in their appearances? I can tell you about *one* of them.

Jill had a great figure. But she had one recurring problem: she had what has been termed by some as "saddle bag" thighs, the kind that seem to jiggle when you walk. If you've had the problem, you know what a challenge it can be to get rid of it. Read on: there's hope!

Jill had been touring abroad, and when she came home she had only two weeks to prepare for the pageant that she was scheduled to enter. She felt pretty confident in most areas, but knew she had to do something about tightening and toning those saddle bags. Her solution: use the rebounder. She jogged every day for about twenty minutes; then she sat on the unit and bounced for a few minutes as well.

Did she get results in two weeks? Every bit as much as she had hoped. When pageant time came, Jill's upper legs and buttocks had nary a single jiggle. She smiled with confidence all through that pageant, knowing she looked her best. (An added benefit of her rebounding, Jill found, was that the exercise toned down her appetite, making it easy for her to control her overall weight.)

How to get Jill's success for yourself? Just do what she did—jog a little longer than usual each day. That's all it takes. While the rebounder tones and conditions your whole body, it also concentrates on those problem areas where you need it most.

Now, if you want to add a little more variety to what you're doing, you might try these two exercises along with your jogging: the Fling and the Side Kick. These exercises are *not* designed to make your workout *harder*, only more beneficial and more fun.

The Fling: Begin with a low jog. Then bring one leg up, bend the knee, and point the toe inward toward your other knee. Repeat with the other leg. Try to raise your toe higher each time. Once you get a good rhythm going, you just might imagine yourself doing the Highland Fling on the wind-blown moors of Scotland! Close your eyes: feel the breeze? Smell the fresh-cut hay in the farmers' fields? Hear the bleating of the sheep? You've got it! Keep up the good work!

Side Kick: Jog slowly until you have a good rhythm going. Then alternately raise one leg, then the other, kicking out to the side each time. Keep this up for several minutes. As well as trimming the thighs, this exercise is good for trunk and hip muscles.

Continue with this program and before you know it, those "saddle bags" will be right back where they belong—on the horses and not on you!

To do the Fling, get into a jogging
rhythm, bring one leg up, bend the knee,
and point the toe inward toward the other
knee. Repeat with the other leg.

The Knee Walk helps to trim the thighs.
Simply kneel on the mat and walk in place
on your knees.

81

To perform the Side Kick, begin jogging, then alternately raise one leg, then the other, kicking out to the side each time.

The Bicycle is also good for thighs. Sit in the center of the rebound unit with your heels on the floor, held close together. Begin bouncing, then bring the legs up and work them in a pedaling motion.

82

The Low Jog, simply jogging on the mat, is good for all body toning and trimming needs. The thighs are no exception.

Slimming the Waist

Think about it: which of all your measurements makes the most difference in whether or not you have a pleasing figure? The answer: the waistline. With a small waist, there is a nice contrast in the curves of our bodies; with a thick waist—well, the outline is pretty much straight up and down, and what kind of a figure is that? There aren't many curves! And curves are what *makes* a woman's figure.

Some women are resigned to the shape they have now. But they don't have to be. Because, along with everything else, the rebound unit is good for waist problems, too.

Let me tell you about Lillian W. She was quite a bit overweight; her waist had become so thick that it was even difficult for her to bend over to tie her shoes. Her problem was further complicated by recurring bouts of indigestion due to stress.

Lillian began a rebounding program and with simple jogging—and no dieting—she lost seven pounds in six weeks. This is not a great amount, to be sure, but it was very encouraging to Lillian. It gave her motivation to move ahead. Soon she had lost four inches in her waist. Perhaps as gratifying as losing those inches was the fact that Lillian also lost her indigestion! Her exercising seemed to do as much for her emotional state as it did for her physical one:

as she continued the rebound program, the feelings of stress were eliminated and along with them went the stomach problems—both internal and external.

Because of its great versatility, rebounding is a unique way to slim your waist. The twisting and turning-type exercises that really work on whittling down the waist are possible on the rebound unit without the trauma to knees and legs and other parts of the body that occurs when performing these same actions on the floor.

Here are a few you can try:

The Bounce Twist consists of twisting your body from side to side while jumping on the rebound unit. Be sure your body from the waist up is turned in the opposite direction of your body from the waist down. In other words, point your arms to the left when your knees and feet are pointed to the right, and vice versa. With each bounce, twist your body in the opposite direction from which it was pointed before. You should be able to feel your waistline being twisted and pulled—it's a good feeling.

A variation of this is to do the old Twist dance—Chubby Checker style—without the bouncing. The advantage to doing this on the rebound unit is that there is less friction on your feet than there would be on the floor and you can get as carried away as you want to—go ahead, feel like a kid again!

Another exercise you'll want to try is the Sitting Bounce: Just sit in the middle of the rebound unit and bounce up and down, using both arms and legs to lift you off the mat. As your stomach muscles strengthen, begin raising your feet off the floor, so that your arms and stomach do all the lifting work. This works on all the muscles of the stomach area as well as your waist.

As with most of the other specialized exercises outlined in this book, these are suggested merely for variety's sake. You can get the slimming-down effects in your waist simply by jogging on the rebound unit. The jogging by itself will burn the fat deposits away and will cause great changes to take place. But these other exercises will further the toning process—and make what you're doing more fun. Just as variety is the spice of life—so it is with exercise.

Get into a program of regular rebounding exercise, and stay there, and before you know it you'll be getting compliments about your slender waist.

The Jumping Jack is a good exercise for the waist. Jump up and down on the rebound unit performing the popular calisthenic, the jumping jack. Start by standing on the unit with arms at your side and feet together. Jump upwards, touching your hands over your head. Return to the starting position and repeat with a rhythmic bounce.

To do the Bounce Twist, jump on the rebound unit and twist your body from side to side. Turn your body from the waist up in the opposite direction of your hips and legs. With each bounce, twist back the other way.

The Sitting Bounce is done by sitting in the middle of the rebound unit and bouncing up and down, using your arms and legs to lift you off the mat. As your stomach muscles grow stronger, raise your feet off your floor, making your arms and stomach muscles do all the work.

The Low Jog, simply jogging on the mat, is good for all body toning and trimming needs, including the waist.

Conditioning Sagging Arms

Perhaps one of the most unattractive things on a woman is that saggy, baggy flesh under her upper arms and behind her shoulders. You know—those folds that bulge from below her sleeves and around the bra straps beneath the back of her dress. I don't suppose that "look" will ever be "in"—and there *is* something you can do about it *with rebounding!*

Now don't be skeptical—jogging on the rebound unit *will condition your arms.* . There are several reasons for this: First of all, you do move your arms when jogging and that's good to begin with. Secondly, rebounding removes excess fluid in the tissue spaces underneath the skin, which is an action that takes place as a result of activating the lymphatic system. And thirdly, because of G-force action on the skin and muscles (see "How Does Rebound Exercise Work—and Why?), these are forced to tighten and become strengthened, toned, and conditioned.

How do you take advantage of the rebound action to condition your arms? First of all, while you jog, make sure that your arms are involved (but easy does it!)—move them, flex them, float them out to the side, out in front, extended toward the back. Feel the pressure that bouncing exerts on your outstretched arms? It's not comfortable to hold them

88

up for long, is it? Be patient. With time you will see a great improvement in your ability to keep them up, and with that improvement will come the strengthening and conditioning you seek.

A second exercise, and even better than simply holding your arms out to the sides, is to rotate your arms in small circles at shoulder height while bouncing. Having your arms in different positions with each bounce this way exerts different forces on each muscle at each point, thus strengthening them even further. You may feel a bit uncoordinated at this until you get used to it, but it's certainly effective at achieving results. Besides strengthening arm muscles, this exercise relaxes shoulders, neck, and chest.

A third exercise you might like to try is the old elbow push. Bend arms at shoulder height with fingertips touching in front of you. Then while bouncing, push the elbows back and try to make your shoulder blades touch each other. Return arms to the front again, then repeat the elbow push back. Do this rhythmically several times and feel the chest muscles being strengthened as well as the arm muscles.

Many people think the rebound unit is just a jogging machine and that it benefits only the legs and/or the cardiovascular system. These same people are very pleasantly surprised to find that rebounding works for their *whole bodies*. They receive benefits—such as to their arms—that they never dreamed they would. So how about you? Try it—I think you'll like it.

Arm Rotations are effective for conditioning sagging arms. Hold the arms outstretched, parallel to the floor, and rotate them as you jog or bounce.

The Elbow Pull is excellent for sagging upper arms. As you bounce, grasp your hands together and pull.

The Elbow Push is another arm conditioner. As you bounce, put the palms of your hands together and push.

91

Rebound Exercise Can't Really Improve This Saggy, Wrinkled Face and Neck of Mine—Can It?

Why not? If you have a unit, just get on it for a few minutes right now and bounce a little. Concentrate on the way your face feels: can you sense the skin being massaged and the muscles flexing with each bounce? Concentrate, too, on the way your neck feels: tighter? firmer? is it being pulled and strengthened as well?

I'll tell you—rebounding really can improve the face and neck. Let me tell you my own experience, and I think you'll be convinced. (When the rebound unit helped my face, it was a side benefit I never dreamed I'd have. At the time, I didn't even know it was happening!)

When I was a child I was involved in an accident that left me with a long scar on my face. Fortunately this scar follows that fold that we all have from the side of the nose down to one corner of the mouth, so it is not highly noticeable—but it definitely is there and visible. I was able to live with my scar while I was younger, but as I got older, my skin began to droop. One day I looked in the mirror and saw that with the drooping skin on my face, my scar was beginning to fold under and become much more noticeable.

About this time I began to use a rebound unit. I wasn't thinking at all about my sagging face, but about the rest of me! During my first three months on the rebound unit, people kept coming up to me to compliment me on my appearance. They'd even say things such as "your face looks better." The compliments made me feel great! But I assumed that my face was just a little thinner because I'd been rebounding and was simply in better shape all over.

Their comments about my face didn't really sink in by themselves, even when they made specific remarks about my skin color looking rosier. Then one morning I was looking in the mirror and happened to notice that old scar—something had happened to it! Instead of protruding downwards as it had done the last few years, it had actually *lifted*! The skin was tighter and the scar was smoothing out rather than looking puffy as it had before. I was elated! Maybe old age didn't have to come after all!

Without even knowing it, while I was conditioning and toning and firming up other muscles and tissues in my body, I had been doing the same thing for my face. It was a wonderful side benefit—a literal face-lift!

Rebound exercise does improve face, chin, neck, sagging skin, and complexion. I know because it's done exactly that for me, as well as for others I know: Sagging skin takes on new resilience and color, complexions just look healthier and more alive.

Let me tell you how I think it works:

When you rebound, your skin is massaged—up and down, up and down. This gets the circulation going in those layers of skin. As the circulation improves, the waste products that need to *come out* of the skin and the good oxygen and nutrients that need to *go in* are able to flow much more effectively. The whole system works better. Impurities are moved out and new life and color enter in. Any beautician will tell you that facial massage is one of the best ways to keep your skin youthful and healthy-looking. And this is exactly the function that rebounding performs for your face.

Besides improving circulation, rebounding gets rid of those fat deposits under the skin which cause the skin to lose its shape in the first place. Further exercise then tightens up that formerly loose skin to its proper form.

93

Also, because of the acceleration and deceleration of the bouncing movement, each cell becomes conditioned and more firm—and that applies to skin cells as well as muscles.

Here's the program I recommend:

- First of all, be sure to use the rebound unit *daily*. Consistency is the most important ingredient to any health plan.

- Next, while you are bouncing lightly, rotate your head from side to side and up and down to be sure you are getting the full range of movement possible in this area of your body.

- While you're bouncing, pull faces—any kind of funny face—to loosen up and exercise those muscles.

- Use isometric exercises to work on the neck and chin: While you're still bouncing, push with the heel of your hands against your forehead, and push back against them with your forehead—feel that? It's good for you! Repeat this on both sides of your head. Don't get a headache, now; just do it enough to feel good.

Be consistent, keep it up, and you will see improvements—then you'll find yourself smiling in that mirror more and more. (That's what I did!) And what better beauty aid is there for anyone's face than the smile that comes from feeling good about yourself!

Goodbye, Colds and Flu

For fifteen years Richard L. had worked at a desk job. His life was quite sedentary—about the only exercise he got was bowling, noontime walking, and winter skiing (preceded by several weeks of calisthenics). As the years accumulated, his resistance to sickness dropped lower and lower. His sick leave record became so bad that it embarrassed him. In 1978, for example, he missed an average of more than a day a month from sickness, mainly cold- and flu-type ailments.

Finally he decided he'd better make some changes in his life. In April 1979 he began jogging. Eventually he worked up to a four-mile run two to three times a week. And he started to miss less and less work. But in April 1980 he injured his knee and was unable to run anymore. His sick leave record for the remainder of that year was worse than it had been before.

When he heard about rebounding, he decided to give it a try. It couldn't be as good as jogging, he thought, but it might help. He started using his rebound unit fifteen to twenty minutes a day, and after three weeks began to feel stronger.

Now Richard reports that his first six months of rebounding has been the healthiest period he's had in many years. No more colds or flu! In fact, he says, "This is the first time in well over ten years that I've gone over six months without any sickness!"

In the section on how rebounding cleans the cells, I told about my husband's experience with colds and flu. When he felt flu symptoms coming on, he decided to do his rebounding exercise anyway. He was pleased when he never did get the flu that was going around—and that was trying to get him!

Now my husband does this every time he feels a cold or the flu coming on. Usually it works like a dream—or if the illness does succeed in the attack, it is much, much less severe than in times past. I've tried it too, and it really does seem to work.

We have a friend who says the same thing—a friend who is remarkably healthy and seems hardly ever to be ill.

"Why are you always so healthy, Alan?" we asked him one day.

Alan's answer: "Whenever I feel a cold or anything else coming on, my first reaction has always been to get out and get going in some form of exercise, rather than *take it lying down* as most of us do." He swears that his colds are either chased right away or are very mild compared to most of the people he sees. And we believe him!

Mild, invigorating exercise like rebounding can help the body stay free of colds and flu. I'm not saying, of course, that you will never come down with these ailments. And if you do come down with something serious, vigorous exercise may make matters worse. If you feel you're getting something beyond the usual winter cold or flu, you'd probably be wise to see your doctor *before* you try to administer your own remedies.

In general, however, a good health program, which includes exercise, will enable the body to rid itself of harmful wastes. As you keep the good circulation going, you'll be able to "put up a good fight" and ward off these infections. You'll likely be much healthier than you were before, and you'll catch fewer illnesses than those who don't exercise to keep up their defense.

So when you see that cold coming, don't surrender without a fight. You may just win the war!

Sleep Better Starting Today

Think about it for a minute: how do you sleep after a day of doing nothing but relaxing, lying around, taking it easy? And how do you sleep after a day of hard physical and/or mental work? When I work hard during the day, I sleep like a log that night. In the same way, **rebound exercise helps people sleep better.**

Numerous studies have been conducted on the subject of sleep and sleeping patterns. And although I'm not a scientist, I believe that there are three main reasons why exercise helps us to sleep better.

A little bit of exercise goes a long way toward getting rid of stress. Mental tension translates itself into bodily tension; when we are able to exercise our muscles, they are more able to relax. The reverse about tension also seems to be true: getting rid of bodily tension has a relaxing effect on our mental tensions. Our brain rests more completely.

Exercise enables the body to rid itself of wastes more effectively. Toxic materials, acids, and the like build up and need to be moved out of the system. Exercise helps to optimize the body's natural processes, including that of waste disposal.

Exercise apparently causes the brain to produce and send out certain vital chemical substances. One of these produces the sensation commonly known as "jogger's high," the euphoric feeling that occurs after exercising until a point of well-being is reached. Another chemical is serotnine, which is a sleep-inducing substance produced from protein foods' amino acids. I believe exercise aids the synthesis of these chemicals.

How do you apply these ideas to your own situation? I suggest three things:

1. Find the best time for you to exercise. For some people this is in the morning, for others it is shortly before they go to bed at night. It all depends on what works best for you. If you sleep better right after you exercise, then bedtime is the right time for you to rebound. If exercising anytime during the day helps you sleep better at night, then you are much more flexible in your choice of exercise times.

2. Give your body time to cool down after your workout. In other words, don't exercise strenuously and then jump right into bed and expect to fall fast asleep. Your body needs time to wind down and relax and let those chemical substances take effect.

3. Be consistent in your sleep habits. Most people have a built-in clock that tells them how much sleep they need (some really do need more than others), and a built-in timetable that tells them *when* the best hours for them to sleep are. Learn what is best for you and set your sleeping schedule accordingly. Then stick to it.

Whatever approach you take, I'm certain you'll find what I have: with rebounding I'm able to sleep better than ever before!

An Easy Way to Unwind or Relax After a Pressure-Filled Day

Have you ever felt as if your insides were tied up in knots? As if you just wanted to scream and let it all out? Join the club! We're all feeling the same thing, especially in this day and age of noise and bustle.

Perhaps you're a mother like me, and have to deal with children tugging at you all day long, teenagers who won't cooperate with the simplest requests, and a husband who comes home from work every day drained and irritable—not to mention the puppy who refuses to be housetrained, the pushy salesman at the door, or the car that won't start even though you've just paid $200 to have it fixed.

Or maybe you work at an office or factory all day, and you have to cope with a boss who doesn't care about your workload—"Just get these extra five things done by tonight!" Maybe you commute to work, and have to fight traffic twice a day, dealing with other drivers who believe in offensive driving, wasting time waiting at lights, spending twice as much at the gas pump as you did five years ago—and all the while the tension builds.

"Stress" has become another of those household words in recent years. And it can, very literally, be a killer. Research has shown that an overload of stress can lead to problems as

99

diverse as ulcers, asthma attacks, depression, and headaches. To make matters worse, stress can increase our susceptibility to *all* forms of illness, from the common cold to the all-too-common cancer.

Once again it's rebounding to the rescue! As with many other forms of exercise, **rebounding can be a great stress reliever.** I'd like to illustrate with two stories:

Don is the local religious leader of the church I belong to, and he claims that the greatest physical source of help he has in his pressure-filled life is his rebound unit. All day long he is heavily involved in solving problems of people who come to him for help and counsel, as well as taking care of his own large family. He has chosen a line of work that can be particularly draining emotionally, and then he comes home at night and he's not through yet. There are usually more meetings to attend, more church work to take care of, Boy Scouts to work with—it never seems to end.

Don says that the best thing he can do to get rid of the stressful feelings that can mount up is to pull out his rebound unit and simply bounce on it for a few minutes while talking to his children or his wife. "In my opinion," Don says, "the ability of rebounding to eliminate stress is a greater benefit than its ability to eliminate excess weight or get the body in shape. The feeling of release I get from rebounding is the greatest thing in the world for me."

Case study number two: My friend, Walt, used to sell rebound units. He tells of one day going into a dentist's office to try to convince the good doctor to buy one. Walt had even carried a unit in with him, but the dentist simply was not interested. He had too many things to do, he said; yes, he knew exercise was important, and it was a nice thing to do if you had the time, but he just didn't have the time himself to spend listening to a sales pitch, let alone exercise every day himself.

Walt, after using every persuasive argument he had, finally convinced the dentist to just get up on the unit and bounce a few minutes—just to see what it was like. After a very short time of simple jumping, the dentist's whole attitude changed. "I'll buy it!" he said. "To heck with the exercise—I like the way it relaxes me! After a long day of bending over patients, I need something like this to relax my aching muscles and help me unwind." Walt made the sale right there on the spot.

Rebounding can very definitely relieve stress. Its soothing effect can take your mind off your problems—or relax you enough to work on them calmly and steadily. It can eliminate tensions. It can help you relax and sleep better. Many doctors are now prescribing exercise for stress, with excellent results. Some are even prescribing rebounding in particular.

At two leading universities psychologists are prescribing exercise for depression, rather than holding analysis sessions. They've found that after two months of steady exercise (three times a week), a patient's depression is significantly reduced.

How often have you watched a mother quiet her crying baby? What does she do? She merely bounces the little one gently up and down. That gentle motion seems to have an inherent calming effect upon the body. Rebounding works with this natural principle—only it calms big people!

The next time you're feeling particularly stressful, try this simple solution. Get up on your rebound unit and gently bounce for a few minutes. Take a little while several times a day to release and unwind. You will actually feel the troubles flowing away, courtesy of rebounding; no need for tranquilizers or an expensive doctor's couch. Your experience will probably be the same as that of one mother I know.

She found herself fighting her kids all the time. She yelled at them almost from the moment they woke up until she pushed them out the door to go to school. And she hated it.

"They would never cooperate with me," she said. "I know that's true in a lot of families, but I just couldn't take it. I'd hassle with them until they left for school, and then I'd be so drained I couldn't do anything until lunchtime!"

But things started to settle down when this mother started rebounding. She got up ten minutes earlier in the morning to exercise, gradually increasing the time to twenty-five minutes. This way she'd get a nice, little workout before it was time for the family to get up. And, little by little, she felt her tensions drain away.

"At first I was too tired to yell at the kids after exercising. But then I felt too good—I didn't want to ruin it! After that everything worked like magic: the less I yelled, the more the kids cooperated. I feel more emotionally healthy now than I have for years! I feel as if I'm more worthwhile as a person—and I guess I am!"

Heal More Quickly

After I became converted to the great value of rebounding, I told my mother about it. She'd had some serious health problems, and I wondered if rebounding might help her to become healthier in general. I wasn't expecting a great miracle—but I was thinking a small one would be nice! Rebounding did some wondrous things for my mom. Here's her story in her own words:

"The last few years that I taught school were a struggle for me because my health was not good. And when I would go to a doctor about it, he would give me a routine check-up, then he would say, 'I can't find anything wrong with you, Mrs. Kuhn.' This happened several times, and I kept getting progressively worse. My memory was shot—tired—I couldn't remember a thing; I would get dizzy and woozy and would have to resort to staying at my desk where I felt a little more secure; sometimes I would blank out—my eyes would be open but I'd be aware of nothing! I was constantly worn out. This continued until I felt that I should ask to be released from my teaching contract.

"Shortly after this we returned to Flagstaff [where] I found a doctor who realized there was something that needed to be ferreted out and corrected. After a series of tests he found that I was hypoglycemic and that my pituitary gland wasn't functioning as well as it should. There were other things, but these two were in need of immediate attention.

"My doctor was very sincere in wanting to help me. But after about six weeks of taking the prescription he gave me, I still was unable to resume any kind of a routine to take care of my home or the needs of my husband or myself. And I was extremely depressed.

"Our daughter came to see us and brought a rebound unit with her. She informed me that she wanted me to buy one and use it. I thought this was the most ridiculous thing in the world. What could that little round thing do for me! But she won. . . . I got on it but could barely get up enough strength to bounce on it. Without my feet leaving the mat, I bounced very gently only thirteen times and was tired out; so I lay on the couch to get my strength back.

"After [my daughter] left I used the rebound unit a little each day. A couple of months later my son-in-law saw me, and he said he could hardly believe I was the same person.

"Little by little I realized I was able to do things easier. I could remember things better; I got depressed less often; my whole being was better and I had more strength. Life was beginning to be worth living again! Now, five years later, I am still using my rebound unit." (I might add that when mother and I visit each other, we exercise together. She's nearly seventy years old, but she's able to keep up with me!)

Exercise helps the healing process. **And rebounding is a type of exercise that is extremely effective in assisting healing, since it so efficiently promotes better circulation. Good circulation, both of the blood and the lymphatic system, is the key to fighting disease and rebuilding damaged body parts.** In other words, rebounding is one of the best ways of maintaining good health.

Specifically how does good circulation enable the body to fight disease? Let me list several organs or systems and show how they function through exercise and good circulation.

- **Blood.** This system carries nutrients, oxygen, and antibodies to the individual cells of the body, and carries waste materials away.

104

- **Lymph system.** The lymph glands trap harmful bacteria and destroy them, then the lymph fluid carries them to where they may be eliminated from the body. This system literally neutralizes and destroys the poisons and toxins in the body. Efficiency of the lymph system is totally dependant upon muscular movement (which is heightened by exercise) to function. Unlike the blood system, the lymph system has no heart or other organ to pump fluids through its courses. Gravity is one force for movement. Exercise is another.

- **Lungs.** These organs provide the oxygen that is needed by each cell to perform its function. In addition, the lungs also eliminate a certain amount of waste in the form of bacteria and mucus.

- **Gastrointestinal tract.** Exercise keeps the muscles of this system in top condition, so that the food can be processed and bulk waste can be eliminated properly.

- **Mucous membranes.** These trap impurities throughout the body and enable them to be eliminated. This also requires good circulation.

- **Liver.** Performs about 30 very important duties every day. Good circulation in the liver is of utmost importance!

- **Spleen.** White blood cells—the body's disease fighters—are produced here and distributed throughout the bloodstream.

- **Skin.** The body's greatest armor, the skin protects our internal organs and tissues from disease invasion. Also the body's largest waste system, the skin excretes many materials through sweat and oil glands.

All of these systems and organs work together to fight disease and to help the body heal itself. None of them can function at their peak condition unless the circulation system is working at its peak condition—and that cannot take place without a good exercise program. Rebounding is the best.

What is one of the first things a doctor instructs a patient to do as soon after surgery as possible? Get the body moving. Why? Because exercise causes the bodily functions to resume their working order faster; as a consequence, the body can heal more quickly. This means mild exercise at first, to be sure. And what exercise can progress from mild to active with the least stress to the patient and at the patient's own rate? You're right! Rebounding.

Perhaps you saw the TV movie of the true-life story of Kathy Miller. This young girl, after suffering massive brain damage and a compound fracture of her right leg in a car accident, was in a coma for ten weeks and then revived with no ability to walk, talk, or write.

Yet after five months of therapy, Kathy could swim, run, and was well on her way back to normalcy. *An important part of that therapy was the mini-trampoline in Kathy's backyard.* Regular rebounding workouts helped Kathy regain her health and mobility, and continue to help her maintain excellent progress.

One woman I know encourages her children to rebound when they've fallen or otherwise received a minor injury that would result in bruises. She rubs the leg, for example, where the injury has occurred and then has the child rebound for a few minutes. It gets the circulation going; it gets the healing process more speedily on its way. She tells me that injuries and bruises are very short-lived in their home!

To enable your own body to take care of itself as efficiently as possible, follow these simple procedures:

- Exercise with your rebound unit as soon as possible after an injury or surgery. (Follow your doctor's orders, of course, though exercise will almost surely be part of what he tells you to do.)

- Exercise with your rebound unit to combat colds, flu, and other ailments *as you feel them coming on.* Don't take to your bed, as you'll probably want to do. Take to your rebound unit instead—then you just may not need the bed at all.

- Above all, proceed with caution: do not overdo. Your purpose is to heal, not to aggravate, an injury. Mild exercise to encourage better circulation and help the body's natural processes is what you want, not exhaustion and further weakness. Just as with any other physical treatment, some exercise is good; twice as much is not necessarily better.

These bodies of flesh and bone that we possess are the most amazing mechanisms on earth, and the only ones equipped to heal themselves, at least to a great extent. Most of these healing processes go on without our even being aware of them. But when we do become aware of how much we *can* do to aid them in their work, to keep them functioning properly through good exercise, they'll do even better by us. Circulation is an important key to healing—and rebounding is the key to circulation.

Eliminate Lower Back Problems

"Oh, my aching back!"

How many times have you heard that? How many times have you *felt* it? Aching backs seem to be one of the curses of modern civilization. But now there's hope: **Many types of back problems can be eliminated by regular rebound exercise.** Let me give you some examples:

Many lower back problems can be eliminated by stretching the muscles. Many of us lead a sitting-down life and this position causes the muscles in our lower backs to become cramped and tight and painful. Too much sitting and not enough exercise calls for stretching these muscles.

First of all, try alternate knee lifts: Lie on your back on your rebound unit and extend both legs. Then pull one knee up over your chest with hands clasped around the knee. Hold for a few seconds; lower leg and repeat with other knee. Alternate and repeat several times. (This is an exercise in itself and is also an excellent warm up for the regular rebound routine.)

Also, just the normal jog on the unit, repeated several times throughout the day as a relief from long periods of sitting, will help to loosen up those tight back muscles.

Strengthening abdominal muscles often relieves back pain. Many people don't realize how much the lower back and abdominal muscles coordinate with each other. When the abdominal muscles are out of shape, the lower back muscles try to compensate, giving them more than their fair share of work. No wonder they hurt! Toning up those abdominal muscles, making them do their part in keeping internal organs in line, takes a great deal of pressure off the lower back and even helps support the back.

How to firm up the abdomen? First of all, there is the normal, everyday rebound program. Jogging itself is an exceptionally good program for firming up the abdominal muscles; the action of lifting the legs increases abdominal strength. So jog away—the higher the leg lift the better. (See also sections on trimming waist and stomach.)

A good basic exercise for the abdomen is the Pelvic Tilt. Lie on your back on the rebound unit with knees bent. Tighten the buttocks, then the abdomen as well. Press your lower back into the rebounder mat; hold for several seconds. Repeat several times. Next, while buttocks and abdomen are tightened, raise buttocks a couple of inches off the mat; hold for several seconds. Relax and repeat several times.

Another exercise you'll want to try is the Partial Situp. Lie on your back on the unit, with knees well bent. Tighten the abdomen, then slowly raise head and shoulders, and extend hands to knees. Keep the lower back as flat on the mat as possible. Hold for several seconds. Relax and repeat several times.

Strengthening other muscles in the body helps alleviate back pain. As with the abdominal muscles, the job of other muscles in the body is often related to that of the back. Rebounding tones, strengthens, and firms every muscle in your body; therefore, all of those separate parts can work better together. So again, just your usual basic program on the rebound unit will help tremendously in your general well-being, as well as treating specific problems such as those of the lower back.

One word of caution: If you have a ruptured disc or other serious back problems, be sure to bounce *gently* on your rebound unit. Proper rebounding itself should not cause anyone to develop a serious back problem; in fact, rebound exercise cushions and *lessens* most skeletal injuries. So don't fear that rebounding will cause an injury, but do take extra care in any exercise program *not to aggravate* a problem that already exists.

There is almost nothing as incapacitating as an aching back, so take good care of this area of your body. Here especially, an ounce of prevention is worth a pound of cure.

Get Your Heart in Shape Before It's Too Late

Almost everyone is aware that the first thing doctors tell heart attack victims is to start exercising in order to build up the condition of their hearts. The patients may begin by walking short distances, then longer distances. Gradually, they'll move into a program of slow jogs.

A gentleman from California writes, "I had open-heart surgery termed 'sextuple bypass.' . . . and returned to normal activity as an electrician. . . . But I soon discovered that I had no time to continue my usual five miles of running daily and felt quite desperate when pain resulted from my inactivity." His doctor advised him to exercise more—but he was frustrated until he discovered rebounding. "What a blessing! Now I not only get my required exercise, but I accomplish it by a *safe* jogging motion which I do at *my* convenience. . . . I am happy to report that I have lost 21 pounds and have no more pain in my legs.

"I am now looking forward to telling my other heart surgery friends about it."

After years of living an unhealthy lifestyle—high cholesterol diet, heavy smoking, overweight, no exercise—Rollin K. suffered two heart attacks six months apart. Consultation with a cardiologist brought a recommendation of a triple coronary artery bypass, a procedure Rollin greatly hesitated to undergo.

Instead he asked for medication and significantly improved his diet and exercise programs. He lost weight and stopped smoking. In two years he went from a state of only being able to exercise 3.2 minutes before having to stop from heart pains to being able to run and walk four miles five times a week. He also quit taking the medication—and was diagnosed as no longer needing a bypass.

Rollin was able to gradually increase his walking distance from his home; at first only able to go 200 yards before experiencing pain, he ended up being able to go four miles. But Rollin was unusual. Many patients lack either the stamina or the courage to venture away from their homes—where they know they're closer to help—even in order to get the exercise they need in overcoming their heart problems. What is the answer for them—indeed, what might Rollin Kimball have tried rather than risking a heart attack when he was a distance from his home?

Rebound exercise is one of the best for heart conditioning.

Why is this so?

- You can begin a very slow, gentle basic jogging program on a rebound unit. Most people's minds become so enthusiastic about beginning an exercise program that they force their bodies to follow that enthusiasm—and do too much too soon, resulting in *damage* to their hearts rather than *good*. If a person has experienced heart trouble, *it is of the utmost importance to begin slowly*. This way the heart is conditioned *slowly,* and is gradually able to handle more and more stress—which means it has become stronger.

- Rebounding is very safe. As I have already mentioned, few things are more frightening than being away from telephone or loved ones when a heart attack strikes. You can rebound in your own home, where you can get immediate help if necessary; there is no need to turn around and walk the block or two *back* before you reach the help you need.

112

- The ratio of results received to time spent is very favorable. Compare rebounding to walking or jogging: the results are as great or greater for the time you invest. *Plus* you are receiving help not only to your heart, your cardiovascular system, but to *your whole body* when you rebound; the parts and the whole are served at the same time. What could be better?

Because of these factors, many doctors are now recommending rebound exercise over any other form of exercise for their heart patients.

I'd like to give you one more example that demonstrates that rebound exercise is the *best*—most beneficial—form of heart exercise. Most people know that postal carriers get in lots of walking everyday. They are a healthy bunch in many ways because of the exercise they get—the very exercise many doctors recommend for a healthy heart. I happen to know a postman (age 36), who uses his rebound unit every day *in addition* to his regular walking. Why? You would think that he'd be in good enough shape already. Not so, he says. His body was in good condition because of the walking, yes, but he was not receiving the aerobic training effect that his heart needed.

His calculations told him that his pulse should be 130 for a training effect—and walking didn't bring it up that far. He used his rebound unit to get that heart rate up to where it was giving him the conditioning treatment his body needed. *It was the overall conditioning and increased circulation he was looking for*—which only the rebound action could give him.

If a man who walks for a living feels a need for more, what does that say about the rest of us?

Exercises for Varicose Veins, Phlebitis, and Other Blood Circulation Problems

Many doctors call our legs our "second heart." The circulation in our legs is vitally important to the circulation in the rest of our body—in fact, for many years now, the medical profession has recommended walking and other similar forms of exercise for those with circulation problems. Just the simple motion of walking—getting the legs moving—acts as a pumping movement to get the blood going up and down through the veins and arteries as it should.

It shouldn't be surprising, then, that growing numbers of physicians are recommending rebounding *in particular* for patients afflicted with varicose veins, phlebitis, and other related problems. **I believe rebound exercise to be the very best exercise available to improve circulation, at least for the great majority of people.** Rebounding is very convenient, and it's *easy* for people to just pull out their rebound units and gently walk or jog on them. At the same time, rebound exercise is easier than jogging or walking on the joints and muscles (about 85 percent easier), eliminating a lot of the problems you get with other kinds of exercise.

I have received information from many doctors about rebounding, and, in the process, I've been able to gather testimonials from many of their patients. These testimonials tell of the superior effectiveness of rebounding, particularly pertaining to circulatory problems. But instead of recounting all those stories, let me simply tell you the story that I know best: my own.

When I was a young thirteen-year-old, I was in an auto accident and was briefly paralyzed from the waist down. The paralysis disappeared in about three days, but it left behind an awful legacy: severe varicose veins.

Most people know how unsightly varicose veins can be. But those who have suffered from them know there is something much worse than the appearance, and that's the terrible pain this ailment brings. I don't know how to describe the constant, unyielding misery that comes with this affliction. It hurt so bad I even had to have some of my veins dissolved, in order to get rid of some of the pain. Even then much of the suffering—as well as the ugliness—remained. Imagine how I felt as a teenager!

At the time of my marriage, the self-consciousness was very much with me. I sought every answer I could for my problem, and finally embarked on a nutritional regimen, which I personally credit for an improvement in my venous problem. At least the pain subsided. But with my first three pregnancies, the veins became progressively more unsightly.

At the time of my last pregnancy, when I was thirty-two years old, the doctor was very concerned about my condition. He even wanted to operate and strip my veins, but I was unwilling to go through with it. He prescribed a special elastic stocking, which I was to put on every morning before getting out of bed, *before* the blood could fill up those veins. I also walked and exercised as much as I could and followed a disciplined nutritional program. After the baby was born, the doctor, upon examining me, was surprised at how well I had come through the ordeal and at the fact that the veins had not become worse than before.

At this time I didn't own a rebound unit, but a physical therapist friend who shared my concern about health convinced me that I should buy one—one of the first on the market. This was my first exposure to rebounding—and I'll always be grateful to my therapist friend for encouraging me to persist in her prescribed rebound program.

Can you imagine the joy I felt as I began to notice a very definite change in my ankles? The veins were becoming lighter in color! Many had been so severe that they were nearly black—but those were now changing to purple. Soon the purple became violet, the violet changed to scarlet, then red, then at last a mere pink! My varicose veins never disappeared completely, unfortunately, but this pink was plainly light-years away from their former state.

As the ugliness left, the emotional pain went with it. It diminished until I finally felt like I not only had new legs, but was a whole new person! (My wonderful, long-suffering husband can tell you how for years I struggled with the terrible discomfort, emotional as well as physical. For example, with my concern as a young woman and wife about how they looked, I always covered my swimsuit with a long robe when I was in the presence of others. My husband says that, despite all of the other advantages and positive aspects of the rebound unit, what it has done for my legs alone, as well as my self-esteem, has made the purchase worthwhile. And he didn't compliment me on my legs just once, but over and over! My good feelings about myself shot up like a balloon!)

Now, how about you and your circulatory problem? I know that if you'll just try, your results can be as dramatic as mine were. A mild routine of daily gentle walking or jogging on your rebound unit can make all the difference in the world to you and your veins. Get those legs moving, get that circulation going, and just see how good it *feels* to have this condition alleviated. Not only will you feel better all over, but those ugly "road maps" just may fade into distant trails.

If my story isn't impressive enough for you, read this letter I received from a fellow in Idaho. I think it just about says it all:

"I would like to tell you what rebounding has done for me in the last two months. Last June I was advised by my physician that my leg would undoubtedly have to be amputated, as I had phlebitis and was also a diabetic. . . .

116

"I had been suffering with the phlebitis since 1972, and last spring the leg turned black almost to the knee and a small green spot was developing on the inside of the ankle. It was about the size of two dollars side by side. The pain was terrific!

"Then I learned of a specialist in a neighboring city. After a few special treatments, my leg condition improved greatly. My knee, however, went bad and I had to wear a knee brace on it. I had to use a cane to walk around, and then only with much discomfort.

"In February I was introduced to rebounding, and I bought a unit. I started using it very moderately each night and morning for about two minutes, and within a week I was able to walk without the cane. Now I can walk very normally and am not too limited in my activities. . . . Eventually the black and green color left my leg."

I've met person after person who has gained much-needed strength through rebounding. In some cases it completely changes their lives. This Idaho friend concluded his letter by saying, "Rebounding has not only helped the knee but I just feel great all over. . . . Now life is more worth living."

Arthritis Relief through Rebounding

Arthritis—millions suffer from it, and they seek desperately for relief. That's exactly what a rebounding program can give them. The aches and pains of arthritis will ease away. Suffering will lessen. Discomfort will be alleviated.

Don't misunderstand me. I realize there are many new programs and so-called doctors these days who claim cures for arthritis—and too many of them turn out to be quacks. **The rebounder will not cure your arthritis. But it can relieve the pain.**

At least that's what people all over the country have reported to me. I almost hesitate to mention it, because of all the quacks around. But I feel the stories of those who have experienced arthritis relief through rebounding are worth listening to. Let me share them with you here, and you can decide for yourself:

- Peggy was a young lady in her early twenties. For quite some time she'd experienced minor aches and pains in her joints. Then she started a rebounding program. In a matter of weeks her pains disappeared.

- Roberta, age 35, has arthritis in every joint, which plagued her constantly. She wanted to exercise, and had tried jogging outdoors, but it was too painful for her.

118

Then she bought a rebound unit. She began with a very gentle program, and it helped her limber up. Eventually she reached her current exercise level of fifteen minutes twice a day. "I'm sold on rebounding for arthritis," she says. "I feel better all over."

- Sarah was a 66-year-old woman whose arthritis was so painful that she could barely get out of a chair. After using a rebound unit for two weeks, she was able to lift herself out of a chair with no pain—and could finally get a full night's sleep, a luxury she hadn't enjoyed for a long time. (An extra benefit Sarah says she received from rebounding was an improvement in her eyesight. After continuing her rebound program, she found she was able to read without her glasses.)

- Thomas, an older gentleman, tells his own story: "I have been afflicted with the very painful and crippling disease called arthritis for several years, and for over a year have been dependent upon a cane to walk with. I was advised by my doctors to exercise as much as was physically possible for me. You don't do too much when every move you make is very painful. Consequently, my physical condition continued on a declining scale until at times I was forced to take nitroglycerin capsules to stimulate my heart.

"About two months ago, . . . after consultation with my doctor, I began an exercise program on a rebound unit. It was quite difficult and painful at first, but I had some immediate and positive results. After the first week I was able to walk about without the use of my cane. I was also able to bend over from the waist and touch the floor with my fingertips, a feat I had not been capable of for years. After using the rebound unit for about one month my heart was strengthened so much that I was able to undergo surgery. . . . Since I have been rebounding I have not had to take nitroglycerin capsules.

"I still have the arthritis and a lot of pain, but I am so much more mobile than I have been for a long time. I use my rebound unit every day and am so grateful for it and the people who made it."

I think these stories speak for themselves. They don't claim a cure for arthritis, but a great deal of relief seems reasonably certain. If you're an arthritis sufferer who's tired of phony cures, a rebounding program could well be just what you need. Start slowly—but start now!

High Blood Pressure—It Could Kill You

In recent years public attention has been drawn very effectively to the fact that high blood pressure is a very serious ailment. It's a problem that should be taken care of and watched faithfully. Medication is the usual treatment, but exercise has a significant amount of influence on high blood pressure—more than most people imagine.

Walt is a busy executive who went in for a physical examination in order to apply for more life insurance. The nurse whistled in amazement as she took Walt's blood pressure. "Incredible!" she said. "And you're still walking around?"

The doctor recommended that Walt become involved in an aerobics exercise program. Walt went home and began a rebound program, which he continued for two weeks before returning for another physical. What were the results this time? His blood pressure had gone down sufficiently enough for him to be able to pass the physical and get his insurance.

Walt has continued to use the unit faithfully six days a week and says he feels great—he can even tie his shoes with ease. (Those with high blood pressure know why that's important!) One morning recently he checked his blood pressure before exercise: it was 140/70. After rebounding for fifteen minutes, he checked again. His blood pressure was down to 120/60.

Dr. Herbert DeVries, professor of physical education at the University of Southern California, says, "We've proved that any normal, healthy, older person can regenerate himself to some extent through carefully planned and controlled exercise. *The time spent is short, the rewards are great.* People ranging from 52 to 87, doing one-hour workouts at a leisurely manner only three times a week experienced the disappearance of long-standing migraines, headaches, backaches, relief of joint stiffness and muscle pain; redirection of nervous tension and body fat; *lowered blood pressure;* improvement of heart and blood vessels function and increases in arm strength." ("Rejuvenation," by Linda Clark)

Have high blood pressure? Get on that rebound unit and get going! "The time spent is short, the rewards are great."

Improved Eyesight

My friend Nina C. called me the other day to tell me about her latest visit to the eye doctor. She said that the doctor was very interested to note that Nina had gained considerable improvement in her eyesight since the last visit. "What in the world have you been doing?" he asked. Nina couldn't think of a single thing she'd been doing differently. "Have you been involved in some kind of exercise program that's new to you?" he asked.

"Yes," Nina answered, "just recently I've started swimming every day."

"That must be it," the doctor responded. "The improved circulation from the exercise must be helping your eyes."

Why am I talking about swimming? Because many people have claimed that rebounding has helped their eyesight—and such a belief may not be as far-out as it might at first seem. Exercise improves circulation, and improved circulation can improve one's eyesight, at least to an extent.

One theory I've heard as a possible explanation is that exercise carries more oxygen and glucose to the necessary cells, thereby causing the organ to work more efficiently. I can't answer for the theory behind it, but I *am* certain that *it does work.* Exercise can improve the vision.

I recently learned of a woman who experienced dramatic improvement in her eyesight. Her eyes had been steadily deteriorating over a period of years, but after about one-and-a-half years of using a rebound unit, she saw her eye doctor again, and he was amazed at the positive change that had taken place with her vision. Instead of deteriorating further, the eyes were actually improving! This lady's program on the rebound unit didn't include any specialized exercises; all she'd been doing was jogging and dancing on her unit for up to thirty minutes a day. That was it—and she was experiencing this wonderful side benefit.

Experts seem to agree that when eyesight improves from exercising, the reason is improved circulation. And **there is no better exercise for improving the circulation than rebounding.** Rebounding has another positive effect. Many doctors recommend eye exercises that will force the eye to focus on different things. This is a natural consequence of rebounding. As you are bouncing up and down, your eyes are forced to move, the muscles are exercised, and you must focus on various objects in various positions.

You can capitalize on this movement by consciously exercising your eyes as you rebound. Move them into different positions: look up, down, to each side; focus on something close to you, then on something far away. This is a simple thing you can do to improve another facet of your physical health.

For children's eyes that need strengthening, place a picture on the wall barely above his eye level. Choose a picture of a simple subject, one that's not very complex. Encourage the child to focus his eyes on a particular spot on the picture as he jumps. Some researchers have demonstrated that the moving of the body muscles causes strengthening of the eye muscles.

If you would like a more specialized program involving your vision and rebounding, consult with your eye doctor. Several studies have been done showing the relationship between rebounding and improved eyesight. Perhaps your doctor can share these with you. In addition, you may wish to contact the Institute of Reboundology. Under the direction of an eye doctor, the Institute has developed programs for the improvement of eyesight through rebounding.

How to Kill Your Appetite

Listen to my voice of experience: When people start dieting to lose weight, usually the first thing that happens is that they begin to crave food! The decrease in calories seems to bring an increase in thoughts about food. Well, I have a perfect method for killing your appetite and it works every time!

Five minutes of jogging on a unit, just prior to mealtime, will decrease your appetite. The reason for this lies with your blood sugar level: the lower the level, the greater the appetite—and vice versa.

In his book, *The Overweight Problem*, Dr. Kurt W. Donsbach explains it this way:

"The body converts part of the excess fuel derived from the food we eat to a substance called glycogen, which is subsequently stored in the liver and muscle tissue for immediate conversion back to glucose in time of need. Exercise is a time of need, therefore the conversion takes place then and the blood sugar level is elevated to supply the fuel. When I refer to exercise at this time, I am not talking about a 60-minute tennis match or 50 laps in the pool. I am talking about a controlled physical exertion of from 5 to 10 minutes, no more than 10 minutes before a meal. If you eat at 8 a.m., begin your exercise at 7:40 a.m.

The resultant rise in blood sugar level will decrease your appetite, permitting your closer adherence to a proper eating program."

This explains something that had puzzled me for years. I would notice, when I would visit my husband at construction sites, that several of the men there would eat "like birds" at lunchtime—they seemed to have very little appetite and didn't eat much at all. The work they were doing was so hard and strenuous that it seemed to me that these men should just be devouring great amounts of food at this noon meal. But it was just the opposite: they would have very small lunches and seemed perfectly satisfied.

I see the same thing occurring now as I observe workers in a factory where my husband is supervisor. These men work very hard, but require very little to eat at their lunch breaks. I now know the answer. When they are working hard and exercising their bodies, the desire for food is much less.

This, too, can be the answer for you if you're trying to lose weight but find you're filled with cravings for food or eating more than you should when you sit down for a meal. Keep your rebound unit handy, where you can exercise for just a short five or ten minutes before mealtime, or whenever those cravings hit.

Again, quoting from Dr. Donsbach:

"The biggest question pertains to the proper exercise for such a short period of time. Some prefer calisthenics, others isometrics, push and pull equipment is the in thing now, but I have found the most effective complete body exercise for these short periods of time to be a miniature trampoline. Several models are out and I suggest you investigate the possibility of such a unit. It is readily stored in your home, you need not disrobe to use it, and the medical reports on the effect are extremely salutary. Remember to use it before each meal, if at all possible, and for certain before the traditional large dinner. A side benefit is the alertness and desire to meet daily tasks when you do this regularly before breakfast."

While exercise will not completely get rid of those cravings, when you do sit down to eat or snack, you *will* find that you are satisfied with a much smaller amount of food than you might have been otherwise.

So when cravings for food threaten to take the effectiveness out of your diet, keep that effectiveness there with rebound exercise!

Rebound Exercise Aids Learning and Can Increase I.Q.

What would you say if I were to tell you that rebounding can help you intellectually—that you can learn better and faster when you are engaged in a rebound exercise program? It's true. Please read on.

My son Gary was learning to speedread, an intensive skill in which comprehension at high reading speeds is difficult to master. Gary found that when he took breaks in his studying for exercise every fifteen to thirty minutes, he could comprehend more. In fact, his comprehension rate increased by about 20 percent!

There seem to be many factors involved in explaining how rebounding can help improve learning abilities. I'd like to enumerate several of these for you:

- **Memory curve.** Studies have shown that most of our learning takes place in the first ten to twenty minutes of a learning session; the longer that session extends, the less we learn. By studying for ten minutes, taking an exercise break, then returning to quickly review what has been studied, actual learning and memory is increased dramatically. This is what occurred with my son Gary.

- **Relief of stress.** The idea here is that when we are operating under stress, we cannot concentrate as well and the ideas we are trying to learn are fighting against our other frustrations for center stage. This concept has been studied to great depth at the New York Institute for Child Development, which, in part, treats learning-disabled children through diet and exercise programs—with great success. Chief of therapy Darral Chapman says:

"A great many behavior problems are frustration reactions. A lot of the time these kids are biochemically mad before they are overtly mad. Because of the stress they are under and the pouring out of adrenalin, they are angry inside and look for an excuse to take out the anger—so a lot of unexplained temper tantrums and outbursts are explained by what perceptual and other vision and other problems do biochemically."

The Institute has found that when these children's causes for stress are relieved, scholastic and other developmental progress is rapidly made. What's one of the best ways to relieve stress? Through vigorous, invigorating exercise, such as rebounding.

- **Correction of physical imbalances.** The New York Institute for Child Development works on the premise that an overwhelming number of learning-disabled children's problems are not the results of personality or emotional imbalances, but of physical ones.

  Take John, for example. At 15, John had an IQ of 138—but was failing in school. He was not able to concentrate or achieve. After treatment at the Institute—a great part of which was a rebound exercise program—John's attention span is greater, he is doing work closer to his level, and he no longer finds studying a difficult chore.

  The Institute treats more than 300 children a year from the U.S. and Canada, and has an 87 percent success rate. Since their therapy deals largely with correcting physical imbalances through diet and exercise, rebounding is an important part of Institute treatment.

- **Improved eye/hand coordination.** Many learning abilities are closely related to a person's eyes and hands working well together. One exercise used by the New York Institute for Child Development is that of having a child catch a ball while he or she is bouncing on a rebound unit. This exercise improves eye/hand coordination, and the sense of balance as well.

- **Improved circulation and general health.** When a person is feeling run-down and not in good shape, it is harder to concentrate and be productive. Rebounding's greatest benefit—and the one that brings about all the other benefits—is that it improves the body's circulation systems. The cells then receive the right amounts of substances that they need in order to function their best, and keep us doing our best. The better our brain works, the more we can learn and the better we can learn.

- **Release kinetic energy.** Many people—children especially—are what is known as hyperkinetic: they just have bundles of energy more than other people do. If this extra energy can be vented in some way, these people are then better able to sit and concentrate for periods of time without fidgeting. And what better way to get rid of excess energy than rebounding?

- **Rejuvenate body and mind.** Our bodies are good at storing many things—and harmful toxins is one of them. These need to be eliminated and replaced with fresh oxygen and a new energy supply. Bouncing on a rebound unit for a few minutes will rid the body of waste materials and give you a "clear head," enabling you to go back and study longer and with greater alertness than you had before.

The interrelationship of our bodies and our minds is greater than many of us realize. A good rebound exercise program can be one of the greatest study aids we've ever used. The evidence is building: rebounding *can* increase the ability to learn. And it works for all ages.

Improved Hearing

Rebound exercise can improve your hearing.

Dr. Paul Yanick, a noted audiologist and researcher, has noted marked improvement in hearing-impaired patients who use rebound exercise and who follow his recommended diet changes.

Please understand that I am making no miracle claims here. I don't mean to say the deaf can be caused to hear because of rebounding. But for those who have experienced some hearing loss and other ear problems, improvement can be made through rebound exercise.

For example, many people suffer frequent inner ear infections as a result of poor drainage of canals of the inner ear. A regular, moderate rebound program, by increasing circulation, will enable these drainage processes to function more smoothly and eliminate or prevent infections.

What is true here is true of so many other physical problems we may experience: Using exercise to help our bodies help themselves—to keep the natural processes in peak condition—will not only *restore* us to the good health we previously enjoyed, but will *prevent* many problems that *might* occur in the future.

Rebounding Can Improve Strength

Every time I watch the Olympic gymnastics competition on TV, I marvel at how agile and just generally *strong* the participants are. Most of them compete in events that call upon their bodies to be strong not just in certain areas but *overall*. Their whole bodies are trim, firm, and in impressively good condition.

I don't know if any of those gymnasts use rebounding, but they could. Because **rebound exercise strengthens the body overall.** While rebounding can also strengthen specific parts of the body, such as the legs, for example, its main contribution to your health is that it keeps the entire body in good strength and condition.

This is true for anyone of any age, not just the "younger set," who may still have young bodies but have merely let them get out of shape. One of the most gratifying letters I have received came to me from an older gentleman, Mr. George K.:

"I had viral encephalitis and spent 53 weeks in four separate hospitals. When I was released I was a physical and mental wreck. I could not step up onto a curb on the side of the street. I could only lift 20 pounds up off the floor, and that was very depressing.

132

"I have been using rebounding for about 10 months now, and I have improved considerably. I can now lift over 100 pounds from the floor. I can do 400 sit-ups or more. I can jump up and down with my arms rotating at shoulder length 10,000 times.

"I have come a long way by using my rebound unit. But I still have much more to do."

Isn't that wonderful? Not only has this man regained an amazing amount of physical strength, but along with it he has gained a hopeful, enthusiastic mental outlook: "I still have much more to do," he says—and you just know he'll do it!

And it was his great improvement in physical strength—acquired by using a rebound unit—that gave this man his great optimism and confidence in his future.

Certainly, there are programs and specific exercises that can be executed on the rebound unit to strengthen individual parts of the body. But the greatest value to you will be the general strengthening—and consequent overall feeling of well-being—you receive as you work out on your rebound unit.

How do you get the greatest value from your rebound unit? Just use the two basic movements, the bounce and the jog. The action of these two motions are the best overall workouts in themselves. Every time you go up and down on your rebound unit, each muscle and tissue is massaged and conditioned, all at the same time and in the same remarkable way.

If you do want to concentrate on a specific part of your body as well, there are programs for each throughout this book. Add them to your basic program as much as you like, as much as you need—and while you are toning, firming, and conditioning your arms, your legs, your waist, your thighs, notice how every *other* part of your body is being strengthened as well, without your even having to try.

133

Being More Efficient and Productive

I know we all experience it—that lethargic, listless feeling I'm going to call "afternoon letdown." It comes after you've spent a few hours working hard. You slow down and stop for a few minutes—and then it hits you. Your eyes start to droop, your steps come slower, and all you want to do is lie down and take a nap for a while. It seems like the logical thing to do.

Unfortunately, you're usually not in a position to take that nap.

But here's the approach I used to take to afternoon letdown, whenever I could. We used to have this lovely lazy boy rocker that was just perfect for sitting back in after an active morning. I'd put my feet up, close my eyes—just for a few moments, I'd say, until I get refreshed. But of course it never worked. Those few moments would turn into maybe a half hour or more; and was I refreshed when I got up? *Never!* I was more dragged out than before. And I could forget feeling productive for the entire rest of the day.

But my rebound unit has changed all that! Now, when I start to feel those listless afternoon slowdowns, I get up on the rebound unit and bounce and jog for about five minutes. Does *that* refresh me? You bet it does! I can usually get going right away and put in at least three more hours of productive time that day—after exercising for only five minutes.

When you feel tired, rebound exercise rejuvenates you. Resting is not the answer, even though it would seem to be.

I have my own theory as to why this is so. It seems as though we get going with a store of energy; then after a while the supply becomes "old" energy. It has just kind of stagnated and needs to be gotten rid of to make way for a new energy supply. The rebound unit works the "old" energy out and works in the new.

A more scientific way of putting this is the idea that rebounding gets your circulation going faster; it massages each cell to eliminate waste and bring needed glucose and oxygen to every cell, thereby reviving them and preparing them for further work.

Resting would do just the opposite: It would slow down the cell processes, keep that old energy in, and not do anything to encourage new supplies of nutrients and oxygen, thereby keeping them sluggish and lethargic.

Geri lived in Arizona and had family members in Oklahoma. An emergency arose in Oklahoma and Geri had to be there as soon as she possibly could. She packed, put her rebound unit in the trunk of her car with her luggage, and headed for Oklahoma. Whenever she would begin to feel sleepy on the road, Geri would stop, get out her rebound unit, use it for a few minutes to revive herself, and then head back down the road. She made it to Oklahoma, driving straight through, in time to take care of her family during their emergency.

Then there's Pete. When lunch break comes for him and his fellow employees, Pete doesn't follow them into the cafeteria for a half-hour of talk and junk food. He gets out his rebound unit, exercises for a few minutes, then eats his lunch. Pete feels that he is much more rejuvenated from his lunch break and is able to be much more productive after lunch than if he had spent the time in the cafeteria "relaxing" like everyone else. "It just makes more sense to me," he says. And I tend to agree with him!

How can you use your rebound unit to increase your efficiency and productivity? First of all, establish a good daily exercise program for yourself. A simple bounce and jog routine will put you in perfect shape; improved health will also enable you to sleep better at night, increasing the efficiency of your actual resting hours. Keeping in good shape to begin with is a large factor in your overall effectiveness; getting a good night's sleep is essential to alertness and energy during your working hours.

Then, when those afternoon blues hit—which they always seem to do—instead of succumbing to the great temptation to lie down and surrender (or wasting your afternoon hours wishing you could), jump up on that rebound unit and get rid of them! Get that circulation going, get that oxygen into your bloodstream, and feel your cheeks begin to tingle, your head begin to clear, and your lungs begin to swell with fresh air! You're ready to go again!

Now some people's work *involves* strenuous exercise for extended periods of time, and they may be wise to take a real rest period, one where they actually lie down for a few minutes. But for most of us, the opposite is the problem: not *enough* exercise. And that's why I recommend an *exercise* break to give our bodies the kind of "rest" they need, which is an invigorating change rather than "more of the same."

In very many instances, when our bodies talk, we should listen: they tell us when they need food, rest, warmth, and so on. But, like a wise parent with an inexperienced child, we need to learn best *how* to fill our bodies' needs. And sometimes that "best" is something other than what we perceive at first. Perhaps this is truer in the area of rest than any other. When our bodies tell us to "stop!" in the middle of the day, that may be exactly the wrong thing to do. Instead, tell it to "go!"—for its own good!

How to Calm a Crying Baby

One night Julie S. and her husband were faced with the height of frustration: a tiny baby that wouldn't stop crying. No matter what they tried, she just kept it up. And kept it up. At the top of her little lungs. Walking the floor did no good; feeding wasn't what she needed; changing the diaper made no difference; rocking and singing were futile. Hours later, Julie went back to the bedroom, exhausted, to try to get some rest, while her husband continued the seemingly hopeless vigil.

Julie and Stan happened to have a rebound unit in the living room. After doing his fatherly duty for a while, Stan found himself getting drowsier and drowsier, despite the bawling that was going on right beside his ear. But he didn't want to go to sleep—then Julie might get up again, and she needed her sleep.

Stan thought about it for a moment, trying to think of what he should do. Then he got an idea. He stood up, carried the little one over, stood on his rebound unit, and began to gently bounce. After a few minutes of this mild activity, he suddenly noticed that his daughter was calming down! No longer were her cries so frantic; her little body was relaxing; and a few minutes later she was peacefully sleeping in her father's arms!

Stan couldn't believe it—in fact, he wasn't quite sure he dared to stop. But then he softly walked to the bedroom and laid her in her crib—and she slept the rest of the night through. (And, needless to say, so did a grateful Stan and Julie!)

Since that night, Julie and Stan have used the rebound unit on several occasions for just this same purpose: to bounce their baby to sleep.

When you think about it, it's not really so amazing. After all, when you're holding a baby and he begins to cry, what do you naturally do? Most people begin that gentle up and down, up and down, that bouncing that seems to just automatically and naturally calm and soothe an infant.

"They have a bouncing baby boy," the neighbors said—and they were right in more ways than one!

How to Get Rid of That "Bloated" Feeling

Do you ever experience one of those days when you feel sluggish, heavy, and bigger than you know you are? I certainly do! I feel as though I've drunk a gallon of water and everything jiggles and moves that isn't supposed to—like a "bowlful of jelly." I feel bloated.

The reason for this feeling is that now and then an accumulation of waste materials builds up inside of us; sometimes we refer to it as "retaining water." Our whole digestive tract seems out of kilter somehow. There's only one way to feel better: somehow get rid of that waste. **Rebound exercise helps the body eliminate that buildup of waste and helps us feel better.**

I have the perfect story to tell you about someone who was helped in this area by rebounding—but I can't tell it! The person is very famous, and not too excited about publicity of this sort, so I've agreed to keep the details confidential. I can tell you this, however: her problem was constipation—inability to remove bulk wastes from the system—and the solution was rebounding.

Just as with other organs and systems of the body, the digestive tract needs exercise to enable it to function properly. The digestive system uses sphincter muscles to move the bulk food along the tract and finally out of the body. These muscles, just like any others, need to be conditioned through exercise.

Take bed-ridden hospital patients, for example. Because of their stationary status, many of them lose muscle tone in their digestive tract. The result is constipation, and they are given liquid medication to alleviate the problem.

Bulk wastes are not the only kind that exercise helps to eliminate. Liquid waste elimination is dependent upon a healthy circulatory system. The blood gathers the waste material and carries it to the bladder, where it can be processed and eliminated. The circulatory system also expels liquid wastes through the pores and sweat glands of our skin (which has even been termed by some as the "largest waste organ of the body"). And how do we get that good circulation? Through exercise.

The same goes for that bloated feeling. One of the most effective ways we can get rid of it is rebound exercise. Rebounding will rejuvenate, revive, and energize you in minutes. Instead of feeling sluggish, you'll feel super; instead of heavy, healthy; instead of swollen, sleek!

Exercise for the Elderly or Handicapped

Maybe you have a bad heart and you aren't supposed to run.

Maybe your ankles jar every time you jump rope, making you uncomfortable for the rest of the day.

Maybe you can't afford to pay those expensive annual and monthly dues at your local sports center or gym or spa.

Maybe you're blind and have a hard time finding a good exercise you can do.

Maybe you walk with a cane or crutches and find it hard to do any kind of exercise at all. . . .

Don't worry. If you had all those problems plus ten others just as bad, you could still rebound. Rebounding is the exercise for everyone. **If you can walk, you can rebound.**

A Phoenix newspaper reported: "Esther Delcina Lewis celebrated her 100th birthday dancing a jig on the mini-trampoline in her living room. . . . 'It does wonders for my health,' she said." Esther "sings and dances" on her rebound unit several times a day. An interesting thing about Esther is that she could hardly walk when she started rebounding. She was usually wheeled places in a wheelchair.

Another elderly lady, in her mid-seventies, liked to walk downtown to do her shopping. But as she grew older and older, she became more and more tired, until she just didn't feel like the walk anymore. But after a few weeks on a quality rebound unit, she felt rejuvenated, and had enough energy for her walk, with extra to spare!

A 70-year-old widow had suffered from muscular dystrophy since age 14 and was now confined to a wheelchair. Her doctor told her that if she didn't find a way to exercise, she'd soon be totally bedridden. She was introduced to a rebound unit with therapeutic handles. Gradually she developed the ability to exercise several times a day without assistance. After several weeks of daily exercise, she declared, "I feel like a new person with a reason to live."

Most exercises make you jump and jar, bump your body around, pull and strain and sometimes almost tear. They're uncomfortable, or they cost too much, or it takes too long to get dressed and get going. In the end, a lot of people just give up and don't get the exercise at all.

With the elderly or handicapped, the problems are often even more serious. Some people are homebound, or too weak to exercise, or too limited in their mobility.

Rebound exercise is the answer to all of those problems. It's easy to get started on; it can be adapted for any level of fitness; and it's good for those with a variety of physical ailments, since a quality unit can cushion the trauma to the joints up to 85 percent while the person's rebounding. (Not all units have been clinically tested and found to do this. One major, quality unit has, however. I have personally tested some cheaper units, and I've found them to give a more stressful "ride." Let the buyer beware!)

Beginners can start just by walking on their unit.

Blind people, or those with poor balance, can get support bars that are available and rebound safely with those.

And what if you can't even walk? Rebounding exercise can still work for you. Some handicapped people have received good therapeutic benefits by placing their feet on the rebound unit while another person gently jumps. And some have even laid across the rebound unit while another person gently jumped up and down.

Who can benefit from rebounding exercise? The healthy and the handicapped, the young and the old. Rebounding allows you to take your body *from where it is now,* and to work from there!

Pregnant Woman and Rebound Exercise

Can you continue to use the rebound unit if you become pregnant? The answer is *yes*—if you do it right. A good example is my friend, Irene.

Irene was in her sixth pregnancy. For five months before she became pregnant, she had been following a daily twenty-minute jogging program on the rebound unit. (This is an important point: she had conditioned herself to exercise and so was not beginning something that her body was not already accustomed to.) During the first *seven months* of Irene's pregnancy, she continued her regular program on the unit. Then because she had become heavier and a little more awkward, her last two months' program consisted of a more gentle jog—but she did *not* discontinue her exercise.

What were the results? Irene says, "This—my sixth pregnancy—is the first time I have felt good the whole nine months. I believe that exercise has made the big difference. When I would feel sluggish in the afternoons, I would get out my unit, gently walk on it, and get my energy right back.

"And it wasn't just the pregnancy itself that was better: this was the easiest *delivery* I've ever had as well!"

For pregnant women, exercise on the rebound unit helps

144

maintain good physical condition and makes delivery and recovery easier. Most women know that being in good shape helps them have a safer and easier pregnancy and delivery than when they have not kept their muscles in good tone and condition. Rebounding is the most gentle form of exercise there is and therefore is safe for most pregnant women—not only safe, but highly advisable.

Note this endorsement from Dr. Robert P. Romney, a practicing gynecologist in Utah for over twenty years:

"I heartily endorse judicious, sometimes modified, exercise in the female, be she pregnant or even [having] pelvic relaxation, on a quality rebound exercise platform, which provides the opportunity for adequate exercise with minimal trauma."

He then explains that the "female productive organs are attached rather loosely to the lower abdomen and pelvis," and they are therefore quite free to move with gravitational forces and centrifugal forces. A jumping motion is thus undesirable, since it can put too much stress on the "uterus and other pelvic organs." The answer is a milder form of exercise, and the rebound unit is the perfect place to do it: "I feel that any person who is able to move around can move around on the unit to greater advantage . . . [and] that women who perhaps are not able to tolerate the trauma of a normal exercise program could well benefit from exercising with a quality rebound unit."

So what specifically do you do? Basically, you just continue doing what you've been doing—a gentle jog. Continue with this until it becomes uncomfortable because of your size. After that a simple walk in place for twenty minutes or so *each day* will do it for you. Most doctors recommend walking every day anyway, and having a rebound unit only makes following this instruction easier. To quote again from Dr. Romney: "It is my recommendation to my patients . . . that they should continue with their normal activity and exercise . . . as long as they are comfortable and . . . do not overdo or strain themselves."

Do not *jump* on your rebound unit. This motion is too hard on those muscles that are already stretched. "Just a walking motion, the raising of the heels, bending of the knees . . . provides significant exercise to the person . . . who cannot tolerate any trauma at all to her joints or to her pelvis."

Of course, it is always advisable to check with your own doctor before beginning any exercise program. Every person is different. Knowledge of your health history as well as your current condition are required before *anyone* can accurately tell you how to exercise. (And if you have developed some kind of physical problem with your pregnancy that you didn't have before, you probably shouldn't rebound at all. See your doctor!)

In general, though, if you engaged in a rebounding program *before* your pregnancy and are in good shape, it can only be a great advantage to you. As Dr. Romney says, "I feel, personally, that exercise is an important part for most pregnant women in maintaining *good health, good mental attitude and especially in keeping their emotional status at a high peak.* There is no question that good physical condition aids in the delivery and well being [of] both mother and child."

You've heard of bouncing babies? Now you know they can have bouncing mothers as well!

Sports Conditioning

I am not a qualified athletic trainer; in fact, I'm not even "into" sports, as such. But I've seen rebounding do impressive things for athletes. And I'm not a physical therapist. But I know some therapists who are doing great things for their patients with rebounding.

That really says something to me: if *they*—the athletes—can use it to maintain their hard-won conditioning, then what will it do for the rest of us? If therapists can use it to help people with difficult physical or handicap problems, what will it do for those whose problems are less severe?

Everywhere I turn, such as to athletics and physical therapy, I see more and more evidences of the great benefits that come from rebounding. In order to help you see that **rebound exercise is a valued form of exercise for athletic training and rehabilitation,** let me share these examples that have come to me:

- From William G. Bean, head athletic trainer at the University of Utah:

  "With the treatment and rehabilitation of approximately 400 athletes at the University of Utah's Athletic Training facility any new innovation in helping us condition our athletes during the recovery period from injuries is greatly appreciated.

"We have found the rebound unit to be a very valuable apparatus in our treatment regimen with predominantly lower extremity injuries. The majority of the conditions that sports medicine-oriented personnel evaluate and treat are concerned with ankle, lower legs, and knees. With the reduction of joint trauma associated with running on the unit in comparison to running on a hard surface, we see less joint effusions as well as irritations associated with early rehabilitation of weight bearing joints. [Author's Note: Research shows that our weight-bearing joints receive up to 85 percent less trauma on quality units than they do on hard surfaces.]

"Besides the above-mentioned considerations, the athlete can help maintain or increase his cardiovascular endurance during his recovery period."

• From Richard J. Hunter, Jr., head coach, varsity soccer team, University of Notre Dame:

"[We used rebound units] during our winter preparation season. We were singularly impressed in two important ways: first, as a conditioner, a quality rebound unit seems to hold no equals. Foot speed, power, endurance—these were all areas that were significantly strengthened by using rebounding. Secondly, as a functional trainer the unit was used by a number of our students in heading and trapping exercises. This functional use developed our skills to the maximum in a relatively short period of time.

"Personally, I would also like to state that as a conditioner, I was impressed by the significant improvement that I made in running time, endurance, etc., after having worked with the unit for about six weeks. I find that I am able to keep up with my kids in our running program. That would have been impossible before I started rebounding."

• From the *Sundancer Success Letter*, an encouraging account of diver Klaus Dibiasi's fight to overcome tendonitis:

"Klaus Dibiasi, known as the Blond Angel in his native Italy, has earned the Olympic Gold Medal in Mexico City, Munich, and Montreal for his superb style off the high board. . . . Klaus has also earned a special title among other world class divers, for they have referred to him unquestionably as The Legend. During the Montreal Games he remained cool and poised as a hot, burning pain in his left Achilles tendon made his final hours in competition almost unbearable. He went on to win that day in Canada, but the tendonitis has plagued him since. It looked like the Blond Angel would never again know the unique thrill of the diver's falling flight. Repeated efforts to overcome the nagging problem produced minimal results. It had started at the 1976 Olympic Games and now it was 1981.

"[When rebounding was introduced in Italy, Klaus decided to experiment.] It was certainly worth a try. This just might be the way for the Blond Angel to return. It would certainly enhance the cardiovascular conditioning and breath control Klaus had dedicated his life to. The repeated workouts on the rebound unit brought . . . results that had evaded Klaus since Montreal. He said, 'I feel great, the pain is gone and I feel like I am stronger now than I was, even before the tendonitis.' He looked thoughtful for a moment, then a slow, quiet grin started across his face. We could see the determination in his eyes. The handsome athlete revealed his thoughts, 'It didn't seem like it would ever be possible, but I'll be back,' he said, I'll be back.' "

- And from W. Lee Forsyth of the Physical Therapy and Rehabilitation Center, San Luis Obispo, California:

"A rebound unit has been used in my physical therapy programs at my private office, in the convalescent hospital where I work and at the California Polytechnic University Health Center where I act as Physical Therapy consultant. I can basically state that the main purposes are in conjunction with rehabilitation of patients with muscular weakness, joint immobility, and cardiac rehabilitation.

"I find it most beneficial as a tool in rehabilitating the athletic injuries at the university. There is less trauma to the area involved, whether a sprain or strain, during the treatment phase.

149

"Last but not least, the patients find rebounding enjoyable and fun to use, adding a new dimension to the rehabilitation program of the involved patient."

To me, these stories are most impressive. Here are a couple more that I saw personally:

My son Boyd has used our rebound unit a great deal in our home. It's just a fun way for him to use his energy—but whenever there is any kind of physical fitness test at school, Boyd consistently scores higher than 90 percent of the other children. He just seems to have greater overall strength. I'm sure a contributing factor for this is his use of our rebound unit.

Our neighbor has a teenage son who competes in ski races each year. He began using a rebound unit and told us that he could almost immediately see a difference in his conditioning and the way he was able to compete. When he worked out using rebound exercise he could feel a real change in tone and strength.

Last of all, let me tell you about a twenty-year-old girl who lived with us for a while. She enjoyed jogging and keeping in shape, but developed a severe knee problem; whenever she jogged the pain in her knee was very sharp. She didn't want to quit jogging, but it looked as if she had no choice. Then she started using our rebound unit and was pleased to find that jogging on it caused no pain. She now uses the unit regularly, the pain in her knee is gone, and the knee itself has become much stronger. Now she can even go out and jog on the road with her friends occasionally and keep up with no discomfort.

These are just a few of the examples I've seen and heard. I repeatedly see others use rebounding with great conditioning results. In fact, it is usually the *athletes* who are most amazed and impressed that an apparatus that looks like a child's toy (many of them even call it "a woman's form of exercise"!) can do so much for them. "How can something so simple work so well?" they ask. And you don't have to be an athlete to see that it does!

Improve Balance and Coordination

I get a standard response when I tell people that rebounding will help a person's balance and coordination. The person I'm talking to gives me a quizzical look and says, "Why do I need to worry about that? If I can walk I have good enough balance, don't I?"

"Well," I answer, "that's true. But it's only half true." We all encounter situations every day that require us to use our sense of balance and our coordination to a greater extent than simple walking. For instance:

• Many accidents that happen in and around the home could possibly be prevented by simple improvement in balance and coordination. Slipping on icy sidewalks, tripping over objects in the home—and being able to catch and steady oneself—make a good sense of balance an important asset.

• As we get older and our bones become brittle, a fall can be many times more serious than when we were younger. Ability to maneuver and recover can mean the difference between a serious break or a simple mishap.

• In children, it has been shown that good balance and coordination influences ability to learn, to interact with other children, and to fit in with the activities of the peer group. It is not an *extra* skill to be learned, but one that is intrinsically valuable to all aspects of their lives.

Rebounding does improve balance and coordination.

It's interesting to see how rebounding influences balance. Time after time, people have come to me with the same story: When they began to bounce for the first time, they felt a little unsteady, a little off balance, a little unsure of themselves. But as they continued to work with it, and became accustomed to the sensations and movements on the rebound unit, their feelings of being off balance left and were replaced with confident steadiness. As those muscles were being strengthened, their ability to *maintain* and *regain* balance was greatly increased.

There is something thrilling about a feeling of good balance and coordination. Watch a child's face light up as he first begins to bounce on a trampoline of any kind. When he can control his body as it's being lifted into the air, a delighted, excited feeling seems to seize his whole body. It's the same with all of us. There is an exhilaration that we feel when our entire body is being used and we are in control of it!

Just as satisfying is the great feeling of security a good sense of balance and coordination gives, especially to older people. Many experience such a great fear of falling or being out of control of their bodies that they become afraid to try to do the things they enjoy or go to the places they want to go. When they get that greater confidence in their ability to move and recover, they become freer people, and can lead more fulfilling lives.

What specific things must one do on the rebound unit to gain a better balance and coordination? Nothing special—just the same jog and bounce that is the basis of all rebound exercise. What I mean, of course, is just a gentle bounce, especially at first, using a bar or other kind of support if necessary. As you continue to use the rebound unit, you will become used to the action and the sensation, your muscles all over your body will become stronger and more resilient and responsive—you will be in control and it will feel great!

As time goes on and you wish to increase your abilities even further, you may want to try things such as bouncing on one foot at a time, dancing and kicking, a jump-rope-type movement—anything you can think of that will force your body to be in different positions and require it to recover and balance itself. You will actually be able to watch your own progress. Have fun! The more you do, the more you'll be *able* to do—*that's* the thrill of it all!

The Easiest Way Ever to Increase Stamina and Endurance

Rebounding gives increased strength, stamina, and endurance. The simple practice of going up and down on a rebound unit improves stamina. The pull against gravity that automatically comes with rebounding yields an increased endurance overall. And if a person jogs consistently, giving both heart and lungs a workout, his or her endurance will increase.

A coach at a major university: "I was impressed by the significant improvement made in running time, endurance, etc., after having worked with a rebound unit for about six weeks."

A physical therapist: "Rebounding has been used in my physical therapy programs . . . in conjunction with rehabilitation of patients with muscular weakness, joint immobility, and cardiac problems."

A medical doctor: "Rebounding builds cardiovascular endurance with daily or twice daily workouts. It is excellent for limbering the joints and relaxing the body."

When I first started rebounding I expected a lot of good results, but increasing my stamina and endurance was not one of them. Little did I know that I would enjoy this very important benefit as well. In fact, I didn't even know I'd acquired it! The very pleasant discovery was made while we were on vacation at Lake Powell in southern Utah.

My husband and I had taken some teenagers from our church with us for a few days of swimming, boating, and water skiing. We camped at the same place and swam in the same area that we had the year before. This particular year, as I swam from one side of this lagoon to the other, I noticed that the same distance was far easier for me to swim now than it had been the summer before. I thought, "How interesting!" but I didn't think much of it until my husband went through another test of endurance a few days later. He had become an avid rebound enthusiast, too, and his experience was the real enlightener.

We were skiing one afternoon when all of a sudden one of those fierce, unexpected summer storms began to blow in. The winds were blowing, big black clouds were gathering, and, in great concern for the safety of the young people with us, we quickly began to make preparations to return to the main campground. We tore down our camp, loaded everything into the boat, and headed down the channel as fast as we could to get back to the boat ramp and out of the water.

We made it to the ramp about the time the wind started to hit. My husband jumped out of the boat and ran up that steep ramp a distance of about a quarter of a mile to get the truck. After backing the truck down the ramp, he worked feverishly to get the boat secured to it, and everyone out of the water.

Then, as everyone was safe and he stopped for a minute to catch his breath, my husband realized that he was barely even breathing hard after all of the exertion. He turned to me and said, "You know, I could never have done that last year—and look at me! I'm not even panting! Not bad for a man who's nearly fifty!" It was then that we realized what good shape we were in and how good it felt to be able to do what was needed when it was needed.

As I said, increasing our stamina and endurance was not our goal when we began rebounding. It just "came with the territory." And this same side benefit will come to you as you engage in your rebound program. But if you do want to increase your stamina, there are some specific things you can do to speed up the process.

First of all, rebound *longer* with each workout. Gradually push yourself from your normal pace to a reasonable point—say, fifteen minutes longer than you normally jog.

Perhaps you are recovering from an illness and would like your strength and stamina back. Again, slow and easy wins the race. Start out gently and lightly, then gradually increase your rate. You'll be pleasantly surprised at how quickly you get results.

Some athletes use the rebound unit to stay in shape during the off-season. During the winter, for example, backpackers might use the rebound unit a little longer or faster than they normally do to keep up their stamina for the times when they are able to hike. On the other hand, snow skiers could work out during the summer months to keep in shape for the winter runs. I feel there would be fewer fatal heart attacks among deer hunters during hunting season if they would prepare by rebounding.

Whatever your needs may be, increased strength and ability to endure are certainly benefits we all can enjoy. No matter what your specific reason for using a rebound unit, you'll find that the benefit of stamina will make you feel good all over—all the time!

An Exciting Idea That Brings Additional Benefits

Throughout this book, we've given you ways you can gain great benefits through rebounding. Virtually all those benefits will come simply by doing the basic jog on your rebound unit. But some people may want to take their exercise program even further, adding still greater strength in their upper bodies to the cardio-vascular improvements they're making.

To use the ideas in this section, you'll need additional equipment—but not much. All you need is some *malleable weights* to hold in your hands as you exercise. By holding a weight in each hand as you jump and jog on your rebound unit, you'll automatically obtain greater benefits from your exercise. See if you can find one, two, or three pound sandbags for each hand. The added resistance is the key here. (Some people also use weights on their ankles to strengthen their legs.) And, if you can't find sandbags, here's something that should work as well. Go to the grocery store and buy two one-pound bags of popcorn. You now have precisely what you need: a malleable weight! And the cost is minimal. Use the one-pound weight until you need something more, then buy a couple of two-pound bags of popcorn. When you're ready to graduate to three pounds for each hand, find three-pound bags of popcorn, if you can. Or put an empty plastic bread bag inside a second bag and pour three pounds of popcorn in it. Tie the top in a knot. Then repeat the process and you're ready to go!

If neither of these methods turn you on or you already have small bar-bells, they can be used. Most people find the malleable weights easier though.

Start with the one-pound weights. Use them until they no longer challenge you. Then move up to the two-pound bags and progress on to the three-pound weights later.

Besides jogging with the weights, you can hold the weights in your hands and do arm curls, arm raises, arm lifts to the side, and so forth. Do the exercises in sets starting out with a few the first day and adding more when you need more challenge. Don't rush into it. Go gradually.

Heart Rate Chart

Age	Maximum Heart Rate	Training Zone Heart Rate
20	200	140-170
25	195	136-165
30	190	133-161
35	185	130-157
40	180	126-153
45	175	122-149
50	170	119-144
55	165	115-140
60	160	112-136
65	155	108-132
70	150	105-127

Exercise becomes most beneficial when the heart gets a good workout. This chart shows the heart rate you should have during exercise; your heart rate should fit somewhere in the training zone. Most experts recommend that your heart rate fit into the training zone for your age for at least twelve to fifteen minutes per day, five days a week.

Don't push too fast at the beginning of an exercise program, though. You'll have best results if you start slow and work up. As you consistently exercise day after day, week after week, your body will begin to respond and you'll find yourself fitting more comfortably within your training zone.

For more information on heart rates, please see the section entitled "Important—Read This," pp. 13-16.

Are All Rebound Units the Same?

Rebounding is an effective way to improve your health—and your life. But all rebound units are not created equal. You'll want to carefully consider and compare before you purchase. To help you, here are the questions I'm asked most often, along with their answers.

What are the main points I should look for in a rebound unit?

Basically, good construction is the most important thing in a rebound unit. I'd recommend you look carefully at the following:

- **Frame** Should be made of tubular steel. On angle-iron units, the spring eventually pulls through the frame. Tubular steel, with its different design, avoids that problem. Some of the cheaper units use only one-half the thickness of the steel of the better units, and a man can bend the legs toward the middle. Make sure the steel is of sufficiently heavy gauge. The steel should have no rough edges to cut through the spring cover.

- **Legs** Should have at least *six* legs, so the unit stands firmly and evenly on the floor and has no chance of tipping. If the leg is detachable, a bolt should be securely welded into it—and the leg should screw firmly into the unit. Also, a washer should be in the bottom of the rubber tip, or the leg will wear through to the floor.

- **Mat** Should be made of polypropylene, with polyester thread reinforcing all extra stitching. The mat should be firm enough not to allow you to hit the floor when you're bouncing, and not too firm to give a jarring effect, as you would experience when jogging on a road. Find something of a happy medium that feels comfortable. Jogging on the best units provides as much as 85 percent less trauma to the weight-bearing joints. If the mat is too tight, it may be too stressful on the body.

- **Grommets** Should be made of nickel-plated steel. Avoid brass grommets. Some units have a metal bar sewn into the mat, onto which the springs are hooked. Make sure the sewing is at least five to seven rows wide on the stitching that reinforces the tabs that hold the bar. Also check to make sure the webbing that holds the bar is of proper strength, and that the bar is of adequate thickness to support the weight it must hold.

- **Springs** Should be made of good quality, high tension wire. Too thick a spring will give too stiff a ride.

- **Spring covering** Should be premium, commercial grade of expandable vinyl, rather than thin, cheap vinyl or plastic. The cheaper material won't have any give to it and will tear easily. You may also want to check to see if the material has fire-resistant qualities. Check the foam backing underneath the vinyl—if it is sewn into or onto the vinyl, it will have a tendency to slip away from where it is needed around the frame.

- **Warranty** Check carefully. Some promise so much that they're ridiculous. If the company guarantees the unit for five years to life, the warranty will almost certainly be so qualified as to be useless. Chances are the company won't be around that long anyway. Some guarantees have such a long list of don'ts (or you'll invalidate the guarantee) that the translation is: "Don't use the unit." Look for a guarantee that's fair and reasonable. To give you a point of comparison, I use a high-quality unit from a very stable company. They warranty their units (except the vinyl covers and foam pads) for two years of "normal use."

161

Which shape is better—round or square?

This is a matter of preference. I'd suggest you try both kinds of units and see which kind of bounce you like. If you like the bounce, you'll use the unit more often.

I've noticed there are different sizes—does it make a difference?

This, too, is a matter of personal preference—and also one of the space available to store and use your unit.

Can you offer any guidelines on price?

As with most products, you usually get what you pay for; check quality first, then consider price. Remember, this is a piece of equipment that you will want to use for years to come; it needs to last. I recommend you consider the better units, which usually range in price from about $199 to $299, retail.

You Will Receive
Benefits You Can't Even
Imagine

You picked up this book looking for a way to get great results in shaping up and trimming down. Thousands of people are now achieving what you are looking for. I believe you can find what you came for—and even more:

- You will find that rebounding is wonderfully easy—much easier than you anticipated. Exercising on a rebound unit is a simple thing to do, and it's easy on your body.

- You will find that rebounding is fun. It is a relaxing, calming, enjoyable way to "let yourself go"—and do some good at the same time.

- You will find that rebounding is safe. It's better than diet pills, crash weight loss plans, or other more stressful forms of exercise.

- You will find that not only do you lose weight, but you *feel good*—your whole health and well-being will be improved: fewer colds, quicker-healing injuries—just name it!

- You will find that even your mental health is improved. You will experience less stress—and be able to get rid of it better; you will sleep better; you will learn more, and more easily. You will feel better about yourself—perhaps better than ever before.

163

- You will receive nice comments and compliments from friends—even from some people you don't know!

As you establish a consistent rebound exercise program, you will receive benefits that far exceed the cost of this book. You'll be benefitting from an idea called *gestalt, the concept that the whole is greater than the sum of the individual parts.* Rebounding gives you gestalt when it comes to your physical and mental health.

A common example of this is a bundle of sticks: Try to break each one individually and it's easy. Put them all together and it becomes nearly impossible to break them.

The same thing happens with rebounding: you may concentrate on improving one aspect of your health or appearance—and you *will* get specific results—but at the same time you'll find that your whole body, *your whole self,* will be benefited. I can't tell you why—I don't know why—but I believe that you will feel it and know it for yourself.

- Maybe the reason is because you feel proud of yourself, confident in your appearance and your performance.

- Maybe it's because you will find yourself suddenly with extra time to do what you want to do because exercise is a preventive approach to health care. You shouldn't be tired, run down, and out of condition as much as you were before; that half-hour spent in exercise yields two or three more hours of productivity than you had previously.

- Maybe it's because you will find yourself with more energy to do what you have to do. You can accomplish more with less effort than ever before.

- Maybe it's because problems will seem less traumatic than they have at other times in your life; you will be able to handle more, you won't worry as much, you'll be calmer and more in control.

I believe that rebounding will help you improve whatever area of your body you wish to improve—and very likely much more. You will have such a great overall feeling of well-being and health that you will not even be able to explain it yourself! But you will feel it—what a satisfying, gratifying, wonderful feeling! And you'll feel it every day of your life.!

Join with me, then, and become one of the thousands of avid rebound enthusiasts who have added years of good health to a life that's now happier. There's no better time to start than today!

For Further Information

Olympus Distributing would like to recognize David Hall for his participation in the continued development of the improved tapered springs. We also appreciate his tenacity in teaching the valuable benefits of rebound exercise. Indeed, Mr. Hall has taken rebounding to a higher level than was previously experienced. We feel that through his efforts there has been a resurgence of interest and enthusiasm in this exceptional type of fitness.

To understand more about the benefits of rebounding, please consider the following:

The Golden Seven Plus One, (Conquer Disease with Eight Keys to Health, Beauty & Peace), an amazing book by C. Samuel West, D.N., N.D.
Six videos with Dr. West sharing his findings on blood protein research.

CELLERCISE, from the Center for Cellular Health, David Hall's excellent video on specific exercises for cellular health. View his website www.cellercize.com.

Other information may be obtained by calling 1-800-531-3180.